A Searcher's Quest For
TELESIS

Personal Change

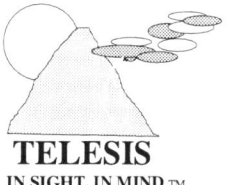

TELESIS
IN SIGHT, IN MIND ™

Visualizing Goals

ISBN 0-9655132-0-3

© 1993 1994 1995 1997 Larry K. Johanson
All Rights Reserved

Dedication

To the family and friends in my life. My wife Arlys, my best friend. My daughters, Melanie, Amy, Leanne, Lyndzee, and Ashley. To my parents, Keith and Grace Johanson. To the memory of my sister, Jennifer. (I will always remember your fingerprint sandwiches) Thanks to Kevin Kunz for internalizing Telesis and for his enthusiastic encouragement.

Foreword

Just as psychology is considered the health care of the 21st century, the philosophy of "Telesis" is the door to tomorrow. The ability to visualize and cognitively conceive our future in a positive manner is the soul of change in our life.

Larry Johanson has the very key to the door of tomorrow. In his inspired program he literally offers this key to those who read his book and follow the directives of his conference.

As a mental health professional I witness each day the benefits to those who are able to mentally experience their future through visualization. The influence of "Telesis" also comes into the life of each workshop participant the same way, directed by the able teachings of Larry Johanson.

I highly recommend the future to you through the eyes of "Telesis."

Ron Day LCSW
Psychotherapist

Larry K. Johanson

When change comes to us, we should embrace it. It often offers new hope and direction. Change is a necessary prerequisite to setting and achieving goals. We must be able to visualize what we expect to accomplish!

Larry Johanson CLU ChFC, is President and owner of Telesis. He received his Bachelor's Degree in Zoology from Weber State College (Weber State University) in Ogden, Utah and taught science in secondary education for four years.

Since 1980 he has been active in the insurance industry. Larry received the professional designations of CLU (Chartered Life Underwriter) and ChFC (Chartered Financial Consultant) from The American College in 1988 and 1989, respectively.

It was his interest in psychology (his college minor) and his practical experience with the motivation necessary to succeed in sales, that spawned the ideas within *Searchers and Telesis*. His "goal books" became the foundation and catalyst for writing. In 1991 and 1992 as seminars were presented, he found others desired the ideas and methods of Telesis.

He formed his company, Telesis, in 1992 and began the process of organizing his ideas and thoughts previously written into what is now called, *A Searchers Quest For Telesis*, a program for those desiring a way to deal with the changes that must accompany goal achievement and the visualization of those same goals. Larry and his wife Arlys have five daughters, Melanie, Amy, Leanne, Lyndzee, and Ashley.

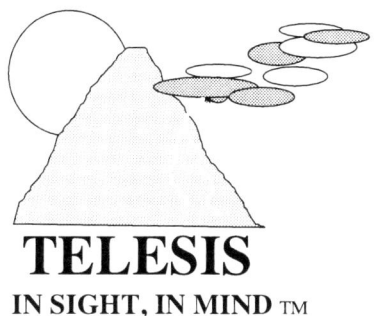

TELESIS
IN SIGHT, IN MIND ™

ABOUT THE "TELESIS LOGO"

The Storm represents the uncertainty and doubt we all must face sometime in our lives. It can be a very difficult and trying time. When our own personal storms envelope us we **turn inward** and focus too much on our own problems. When we continue to "hope" we can move forward. A goal or desire gives us hope! When hope is present, it leads to faith. Faith is the force and power that moves us forward. Without faith we are inert.

The Mountain represents our goals. Many men and women have climbed mountains simply because the mountains were there. To climb the mountain successfully was their goal. Often our goals can be hidden and obscured by our personal storms. These storms may be so intense that our mountains are totally hidden from view. When we lose sight of our goals and dreams we truly are in a personal storm. Are you in a storm?

The Rising Sun represents the hope, the faith, the warmth, and the joy that accompanies achievement. The sun rises in our lives when we are **focused outward** and attempting to help others. A rising sun in our lives will move out a storm. The purpose of Telesis is to assist you to come "Out of the storm and into the Light!"

CONTENTS

Part One

SEARCHERS
PERSONAL CHANGE

The Searchers Dream	1
The Pouches	8
The Lobster	10
The Turtle	14
The Chisel	18
The Fish	22
The Clouds	26
The Money	30
The Wheel	35
The Sun	39
The Friend	43
The Eagle	47
The Eye	51
The Sea	55
The Chest	59

Part Two

TELESIS
VISUALIZATION

Establishing Goals	63
Telesis Components	71
Traps of The Goals Setting Process	73
Personal Awareness	75
Steps of Positive Self-Direction	77
Personal Seeds of Success	79
A Personal Inventory	80
Life Management Areas	82
Establishing Our Present Position	84
Personal Development	86
Family Development	90
Educational Development	94
Business Development	98
Rewards of Telesis	102
Visualization and Icons	104
Placing and Organizing Icons	106
Summation	107
Seminar Information	109

PART ONE

SEARCHERS

THE LESSONS
OF
TELESIS

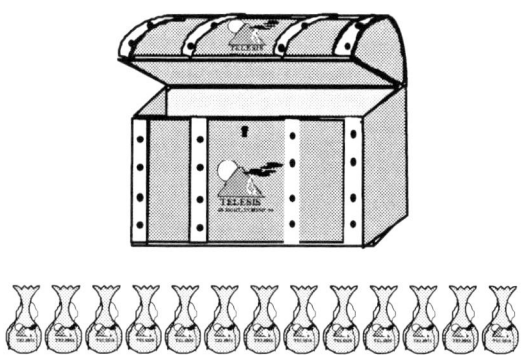

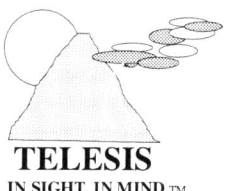

TELESIS
IN SIGHT, IN MIND ™

The Searchers Dream

Ever since the dream I had seen it in my mind very clearly. I could see it in almost every detail. Surely it would be in disrepair, even possibly altered in some manner as to appear plain and ordinary to most who would have it in their possession. Oh, they would use it for many things, and its contents were more than likely lost, but I would see it, and I would recognize it.

The spirit of it, if I can describe it as such, is what I would recognize. After many centuries even its original structure would have been replaced, perhaps many times. I knew, however, that the last person to have it would have laid within it, the contents with reverence, for he or she would have understood their significance and power. I knew from my dream that it was near and that I was supposed to resurrect it as it were, and replace anew the contents that had been placed there so many centuries before. I was to share the dream with others and if they chose to do so they could live their lives in the same manner as those who were taught in times past and gone, and for the times future and yet to come.

The Old Bedouin

The old Bedouin had benefited by it. His camels had carried it many years from place to place as he traveled the deserts. *Its contents had refreshed him and given him comfort as much as any oasis in the desert.* In my dream I had seen him anguish as he instructed his servants to place it within the small vessel that was about to sail. *The contents of it seemed so insignificant that they would most likely not be noticed.* He was saddened by this thought, for he remembered how close he had once come in life to selling it. Had it not been for his dream, he would have done so. As he turned to face his family and those who were with him, *he realized that all that he had become and acquired were very much the result of the wisdom he had gained from the contents of that old trunk.* Silently he said, "Good bye, old friend" and the small vessel departed from the shore.

In my own dream it was not revealed to me how many men or women had obtained by time and circumstance the trunk and its contents. I suppose it has been in the hands of many, but perhaps only a few, the power within lying dormant, and in abeyance until another "searcher" would have "the dream" and be compelled to restore its contents, learn from them, and in time pass them on.

I knew from my dream that the wisdom had been conveyed, since the old Bedouin, in a trunk. The trunk would more than likely be one hundred to one hundred fifty years old. From my dream I knew the contents had made it safely to Spain and had eventually been in the hands of a man who *had desires to be a "searcher," but he had abandoned his hopes and dreams, and yielded to the criticism of family and friends.* He used the trunk only to store what few possessions he had and was unaware of the trunk's hidden contents. Although he had the trunk many years, my dream revealed unto me that the trunk had been sold to pay for his burial. He died a poor man. *Poor in the sense that within himself, he had no center or depth, and he lacked fulfillment.*

Thomas the Seaman

The young seaman thought that a trunk like this would be of much use to him on the voyage to the New World. He was saddened at the plight of the family whose father had just died. The seaman had resolved silently that his fate would not be

INTRODUCTION

similar to that of the old man whose family sold the old trunk that they might bury their father. *Life was ahead of him and he was "searching."* During the long voyage I saw in my dream the young seaman had discovered the contents of the trunk that had been secreted by the Bedouin in a false bottom. The seaman had learned, being a "searcher," and applied the wisdom of the contents in his own life and had found his center and depth. He, too, felt and experienced sadness as he thought of sending the trunk away. It had been his for thirty-two years. A long time to have a trunk! He was concerned that it would sit idle, its contents never revealing themselves. Nevertheless, the seaman gave it to the young man who was *"searching"* for a new place to live with his young bride. They were headed west!

It was not difficult to place all they possessed within the old trunk. The old seaman had given it to the young man for the work he had eagerly done at the docks. Besides the trunk, he had earned enough money to travel west. It was out west that one could find land and opportunity, for he and his new bride were *"searching"* for a better life than most. *Although their decision to leave the comfort and familiar surrounding of friends and family meant some risk, they were determined to search out their special destiny.* Upon their arrival in the Rocky Mountains they had unpacked the old seaman's trunk. A small piece of leather string had been wedged between the bottom and and side of the trunk. The young man pulled the string to remove it and noticed the bottom gave way. In what had appeared to be an empty trunk, was a compartment that contained small leather pouches, each containing an object, and a short story about its contents. The young man and his bride read the seaman's note: *"To the 'searcher' who finds this paper where upon I write, take time to study these objects, for in them is the pathway to your hopes and dreams. April 1847."*

William and Sarah

William and Sarah had accomplished much in their lives. They raised three daughters and four sons. They were ready to retire from the freight business. Their children were all doing well.

SEARCHERS

They had gone off in search of their hopes and dreams armed well with the wisdom they had been taught by William and Sarah. William and Sarah had many times removed the contents of the trunk from the false bottom to examine them and learn from them. *They knew the contents well.* It was time to find, if they could another *"searcher."* How would they recognize this person? This concerned them, for they did not want the trunk nor its contents to sit idle. In my dream I saw William and Sarah place the contents within the trunk and below its false bottom. They wrote their note to the next *"searcher."* After they had done so, they placed the trunk on the buckboard determined to leave it to fate who should find it. They proceeded to town and gave it to the man whose appearance suggested that he certainly could use the trunk and its contents. They wondered, was he a *"searcher?"* Their sadness at the loss of their cherished trunk was replaced by their knowing they had given it to someone whose appearance suggested he desperately needed it. No sooner had William and Sarah driven out of sight, that the man, unaware of its contents, picked up the trunk and sold it to the owner of a store whose sign said, "I buy and sell junk. Old Bills Collectibles Ogden, Utah." Bill lifted the trunk and carried it *unused and empty* to the cellar of his store, placed it under the stairs and closed the small door with his lantern and *the darkness settled in.*

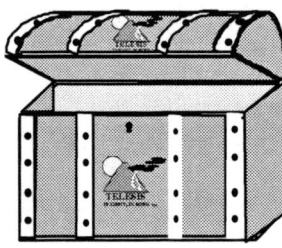

The Old Trunk

It was the next day December 21, 1994. The dream had excited me and I thought how shall I find the trunk. Surely if it still exists it would be difficult to find. I thought to try the old antique stores in the city, particularly those in the old center part of Ogden. I asked each owner if they had any old trunks like the kind which had the dome top. I learned this was called a camel-back type of trunk. Each owner said they had none in their store, but they were familiar with them, that they were fairly common years ago and becoming more rare. I thought to myself, I must be crazy to think I would find such a trunk! After chasing around on what seemed to be a fruitless endeavor, I went to the

INTRODUCTION

Cowboy Trading Post and Antiques Store in the middle part of Historic 25th Street. I inquired about camel-back trunks. The owner, Brent Baldwin, said to his assistant, "Bob, take this guy downstairs and see if that old trunk that was under the stairs is still there. I haven't been down in that little room under the stairs for years. Old Uncle Bill owned that trunk. I think that key there, fits the old lock."

Down the antiquated stairs, themselves covered mostly with various items whose value seemed questionable, and into the basement we went. The dirt floors smelled musty and as if the dust had not been disturbed for years. Bob opened the door to the little room under the stairs and *the light* from his flashlight *pushed the unyielding darkness aside* to reveal an old trunk. We lifted the lid and within it were some old spurs, bridle bits, and a few insignificant articles that at some time must have been placed there by old Uncle Bill.

The trunk looked terrible and surely couldn't be the one I saw in my dream. We took it upstairs and placed it in the light. The contents, the bits and spurs, were removed, for they were sentimental objects to Brent and Bob. I looked into the empty trunk and noticed a small leather string that appeared to be wedged between the bottom and the side of the trunk! Could it be! I could hardly wait to pull that small string of leather, but *I knew that had to be done when I was alone.* After having paid what was too much for an ordinary trunk, I left. I knew this was no ordinary trunk. I was anxious to arrive home and pull the leather string.

Upon arriving home, I secreted myself with the trunk and with a breath deeper than I needed for air I pulled the leather string. It reluctantly gave way with ever increasing ease and finally opened. I noticed a small group of leather pouches each with an apparent individual object within it. Each pouch had an emblem that seemed burned into the leather as if with a very fine brand. In a small water stained envelope was a note. It read: "By studying these objects we have gained wisdom. *They gave us the wisdom we needed before even our own experiences could teach us.* This wisdom protected us and assisted us. We made mistakes in life, but we feel they were less

SEARCHERS

severe because of what we learned from these objects. *These objects have helped us to visualize many years in advance what we have realized in actuality through the passing of time. This knowledge has been the power we have used to reach our hopes and dreams.* Searcher, for we know not your name, when we obtained what you now have in your possession which is this trunk, an old seaman from whom we were briefly acquainted, recited to us a verse in the Old Testament from the Bible he kept in this trunk, 1 Chronicles Chapter 28:20. Be strong and of good courage, and do it: fear not nor be dismayed: for the Lord God, even my God, will be with thee; he will not fail thee, nor forsake thee... God speed fellow searcher, William and Sarah."

The Spirit of the Trunk

I must admit I was very eager and curious to open all the pouches immediately. However, a feeling came over me that I should restore to the trunk as best as I could the dignity it deserved. I had been a carpenter early in my life, and therefore possessed the basic skills needed to use the tools I had collected over the years. The trunk had been painted at least twice before. The metal work had rusted over the years and the hardwood had dried and needed moisture. The nails, square ones at that, were loose. One of the three hinges was gone, and the bottom was weak. It had been through much. If only this trunk could talk! I wiped the dust and dirt away. My effort began to reveal a simple elegance crafted by some fellow carpenter decades ago. Even the smell of the trunk seemed old from the passing of time. There were dents and scrapes, but these were what gave the trunk its character and appeal. Inside the lid of the trunk was a picture of a young woman. I thought she must be in her late twenties or early thirties. She seemed to have dark hair, perhaps black or auburn. The picture, of course, was a black and white photograph. She had a scarf that passed in front of her neck from her right to her left and arose from her left shoulder up and over her head. Her neck was surrounded with delicate lace. Below her chin, a single rose. Was this Sarah? The most striking thing about this young woman was her look. She had the look

INTRODUCTION

of confidence, inner peace, and a certain depth. In a word, she knew fulfillment! As I looked at this young woman, I began to visualize and imagine her sitting with her children as she called them around her. She would more than likely open the trunk and show them her favorite and precious things. For in this trunk she had kept them safe as she and William had traveled West. I was very careful not to damage this simple photograph.

Christmas was only a few days off and it was my desire to make the necessary repairs to the trunk so I might open the first pouch then, and one each day into the new year. My natural tendency was to complete the task as soon as I could. I thought of my own father, however, and realized that if he were here he would exercise patience. He was a carpenter. Carpentry was his livelihood, and he had taught me the basic skills. By Christmas Eve I had finished! I called my neighbor, who had seen the "before," and now I wanted him to see the "after." I did not explain the trunk nor my dream. The finished effort passed the simple inspection. The rust was removed, the wood restored, the metal polished, and the bottom strengthened. Some degree of dignity was restored to the old trunk.

It was most difficult to restrain myself from opening the pouches. I could only guess at their contents. When tempted to open them all at once, I remembered my mother's Christmas as a child. She received an orange one year for Christmas. A rare thing in northern Utah in the 1930's. The orange was her only present. She ate one wedge of the orange each day to make it last. When I think of my mother, I think of thankfulness and patience!

I determined I would be thankful for my dream and the contents of this old trunk. I would learn what it had to offer me, and I would learn it with patience.

SEARCHERS

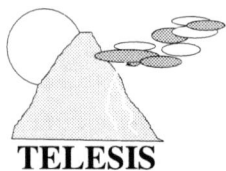

TELESIS
IN SIGHT, IN MIND ™

The Pouches

The pouches were old but well kept and appeared as if they had been oiled for protection against the elements. They were obviously treated before William and Sarah placed them there. Each pouch contained an emblem. A mountain, a sun rising behind it, and clouds moving away with a lightning bolt. I picked up and opened the top of a pouch curious about the contents, for I felt an object within it. I emptied the contents into my hand and to my puzzlement beheld, rolled in a piece of linen, a lobster claw. What possible reason would someone have in saving a lobster claw? I first did not notice the writing on the linen, but when it caught my attention it was fine and delicate. It must have been Sarah's hand. It simply began.

"Dear Fellow Searcher, The paper where upon these parables were written by Thomas, the seaman, have by our reading and re-reading them, been worn out. I have written them upon this linen for you to enjoy as well. The pouches are the ones we received from Thomas. These simple parables have taught us much. Forever, Sarah."

It was enough for now. I was struck with a particular reverence for these pouches. I had previously determined not to open all of them at one time. Rather I was struck with the thought that I should open the second only after I had read the story of the first and eventually to all thirteen. It would be necessary to do this alone and in private for these

INTRODUCTION

objects were meant to be studied and handled with a certain emotion. There are certain emotional feelings that one has when they are "searching."

Having spent several hours over the previous few days reconditioning the trunk, I felt an eagerness to read from the linen. Why had Sarah felt such a necessity to preserve and pass on to the next "searcher" the parables? I was determined to find out, because I myself have been searching, to find my center and my depth.

I opened the lobster pouch and placed the lobster claw before me, unfolded the delicate linen and began to read the story that Sarah had re-written from the papers left to her and William by Thomas, the seaman.

The Lobster Pouch

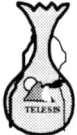 The Master had acquired much worldly wealth. His wisdom was of the greatest value. Master, how can I learn to have my own Telesis for the success I seek? He replied with a raised eyebrow and serious look, **"You must have the ability to see yourself in possession of that which you desire. You must learn to create that which you desire spiritually in your mind, before you can possess it physically. To be able to do this is a great power and talent."**

How shall I learn all that you have learned, Master? I asked. He replied, "For your first lesson toward the attainment of your Telesis, go to the tide pool and observe the lobster. You can learn much from the animals. When the lobster has taught you all he knows, return to me and report your new knowledge."

The waves crashed near the reef, but the lobster's home was in the tide pool where the water was calm. I watched the lobster for many days. I grew weary and returned to report to the master.

"What is your new knowledge, young friend?" he asked. I answered that I had learned nothing from the lobster! The master raised his eyebrow again and seemed puzzled. Then somewhat disappointed, he said, "Tell me what you observed." I replied that the lobster was lazy and did not eat much nor did he venture far from the shelter of the rocks in the small pool. For such a big lobster, he seemed fearful and afraid of everything. The master shaking his head and looking at the ground said, "Tadpole, you must learn to see beyond the sight of your eyes. The lobster is in the shallow tide pool because he is ready to grow. Did you not see that his outer shell appeared tattered and torn? He has grown too big for his old skin, so he does not eat. His old skin must split and allow him to back out of it so that he may again reach new growth. He does this many times in his life. Each time he expects this change in his life, he retreats to the shelter of the tide pool because, for a short time, he is vulnerable to his enemies and those animals who desire to take advantage of his weakened condition. Once the old and familiar is shed, he will experience a new growth. Do you understand, Tadpole?" he asked.

Yes, Master. The lobster was not lazy or fearful, but wise through experience. He knew that when he experienced change for new growth, he was vulnerable, and he sought a place of refuge to prepare for the change. He did not venture far from the shelter of the rock because his eyes were clouded as he shed his old skin. He was alone during this time for he knew that it was when he experienced change or new growth that he was most vulnerable. He realized that his survival depended upon his ability to recognize both his strengths and his weaknesses. He avoided even those of his own kind who might take unfair advantage of his weakened condition. Is this not right, Master? Through the graying beard of the master, I saw a smile. He replied, "Tadpole, you have learned the first lesson which must be learned before you can begin a Telesis." Many times I returned to the Master for his wisdom. **"You must learn to see beyond the sight of your eyes, Tadpole."** How I remember those words! How I remember the lobster!

 What does this parable mean to you? Write briefly in the space below where you are now in your life with respect to the message of the parable.
_____
_____
_____
_____

TELESIS
IN SIGHT, IN MIND ™

What an important thing to remember. **"You must have the ability to see yourself in possession of that which you desire. You must learn to create that which you desire spiritually in your mind, before you can possess it physically. To be able to do this is a great power and talent."**

What was it that Sarah said, *These objects have helped us to visualize many years in advance what we have realized in actuality through the passing of time. This knowledge has been the power we have used to reach our hopes and dreams.* "Once the old and familiar are shed we can begin to experience new growth."

I have had to change many times in my life. Indeed these times have not been easy. *They may have been made easier had I known that when change comes to us, it is a natural part of life.* Perhaps this is what Sarah meant. *"By studying these objects we have gained wisdom. They gave us the wisdom we needed before even our own experiences could teach us."* Sometimes we hold ourselves back because when change does come to us we pull away and fear what could lie ahead. I wonder why it seems more natural to fear the unknown than it is to look forward to it. Why do we often anticipate the worst rather that hope for the best? Perhaps an answer is within another pouch.

How do we move forward with uncertainty? I suppose William and Sarah, Thomas the seaman, and even the old Bedouin faced changes every day of their lives. How did they move forward? It must have been the result of their perspective of life. Is this what they were alluding to? *This knowledge has been the power we have used to reach our hopes and dreams.*

POUCHES

To move forward with uncertainty, that takes faith. Faith in what? Ones self, each other, in the future, or in God? Apparently, Thomas, the seaman had faith. He left a scripture for Sarah and William to find. *1 Chronicles Chapter 28:20.*

Be strong and of good courage, and do it: fear not nor be dismayed: for the Lord God, even my God, will be with thee; he will not fail thee, nor forsake thee... If Thomas truly believed this, it must have given him great confidence and peace. When Thomas or anyone else faced change or needed new growth, this would have given him comfort and courage.

The Master said, "we must have the ability to see ourselves in possession of that which we desire. That this is a great power and talent." So from this parable I have learned to also recognize my strengths and weaknesses. *When I am the most vulnerable I should avoid those who would try to discourage me.* I also may have to shrink at times before I can experience new growth and during these times I may even have to seek shelter in the safety of a tide pool.

If William and Sarah were able to live life with this knowledge and teach it to their children, it is little wonder why they were able to find their center and their depth.

Such were my thoughts as I pondered the parable of the lobster. The next pouch had the emblem of a turtle. What could I learn from a turtle! I placed the claw of the lobster back in the pouch with the linen and reached for the turtle pouch. I would read from it tomorrow.

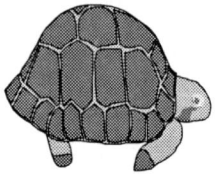

The Turtle Pouch

Master, I have thought about the lobster since our last conversation. It has caused me to consider the way I am feeling. I have told some of my friends about our talk. They think I am silly to visit with you and listen to your stories. I enjoyed the lobster story very much and wish you to teach me more. Will you teach me again?

"If you wish I shall share with you what a turtle knows. Hold this empty turtle shell. *A turtle knows his strengths and weaknesses. Even a turtle has fears.* He doesn't like to climb because this could prove his undoing. Should he end up on his back and not be able to right himself, his shell which had been his protection would become his tomb. His under shell does not offer the same protection from the heat as his upper shell. He might bake in his own home, or because the softer parts of his body are more exposed, his enemies could more easily take advantage of his weaknesses. *As long as he maintains his balance and remains right side up, he is safe.* Even would-be trouble makers like the hawk, the snake, the jackal, the lion, have learned through time that the turtle is a tough nut to crack. He is tough to bite, hard to scratch, and doesn't run fast enough for sport. When trouble comes, the turtle can simply pull in his legs and head, close up shop and wait it out. We can all learn something about patience from the turtle."

Master, how is this story of the turtle important to me? Why have you told me this about the turtle? Surely, if I were to become an animal, I would wish to be a lion, a camel, or the great elephant! Why do you speak so of the lowly turtle?

POUCHES

"Tadpole, the turtle's enemies have learned that to upset the turtle is not easy. To stop his forward progress is difficult. To wait him out is futile. To cause him to panic is rare. To place him at disadvantage is mostly luck. Consequently, his enemies, except for their inexperienced and youthful offspring, usually give him only a passing glance because they have learned the lesson of the turtle."

Master, I am struggling to understand this lesson of the turtle. Will you explain further that the wisdom of the turtle will become clear?

"Like the turtle, we must have hard outer shells against those who would try to discourage and frustrate us. We must have patience when adversity arises. We must know that while there is a time to retreat, there is also a time to forge ahead, even when under attack. When we are upside down, we must work diligently and furiously to right ourselves. We must remember that patience is a virtue when we are surrounded by adversity.

Thank you Master, now I see the wisdom of the turtle.

 What does this parable mean to you? Write briefly in the space below where you are now in your life with respect to the message of the parable.
_____
_____
_____
_____

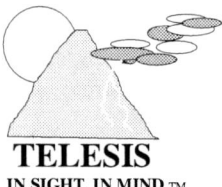

TELESIS
IN SIGHT, IN MIND ™

Is this a lesson that other "searchers" have learned? *I must be at peace with my world and have patience when change comes into my life.* In what ways and circumstances have other "searchers" applied the lesson of the turtle? I wondered as I held the turtle shell in my hands. There seems to be a very simple wisdom in these parables of Telesis. I began to examine the turtle shell closely, really looking at it. I had seen a turtle before, but I had never been able to examine one from the proper distance.

The shell was entirely of three segments. The upper shell was, in fact, one entire segment. The lower shell appeared to be two segments fused together. All three segments joined at a common point at each side near the edge and in the middle of the turtle if you measured front to back. The turtle's back has a box design consisting of ten boxes of various size and symmetry. There were twenty-four smaller box designs around its outer edge. The most striking thing about the shell was the smooth surface of the turtle's bottom shell. Though the designs were visible, they were not as deep. The bottom shell was highly polished and very smooth compared to its upper shell. *It had become smooth through friction and wear as it came in contact with the earth.*

As I held this simple shell in my hands and looked at it from the proper distance, it began to teach me. *If I was to become highly polished, I like the turtle, would have to come in contact with life.* I had to become aware of my strengths and weaknesses. They had to be identified. I also had to identify what interested me and try to move forward in that direction. *Too often I had held back from doing what I really wanted because I focused on the potential problems rather than the likely possibilities.*

POUCHES

What was it the Master said? "*A turtle knows his strengths and weaknesses. Even a turtle has fears.*" "**Like the turtle, we must have hard outer shells against those who would try to discourage and frustrate us. We must have patience when adversity arises. We must know that while there is a time to retreat, there is also a time to forge ahead, even when under attack. When we are upside down, we must work diligently and furiously to right ourselves. We must remember that patience is a virtue when we are surrounded by adversity.**"

I like Tadpole, was becoming fond of the Master's parables. They seem to make it easier to understand the points the Master was trying to teach. The name "searcher" had a meaning, *to diligently seek and to discover,* which appealed to me. *To be worthy of the name "searcher" one would have to accept responsibility for his life. In other words, my life is up to me!*

I resolved to often observe the turtle's shell. It would remind me of the lesson of the turtle. I need only see the turtle's shell and I would be able to remember all that it represented. *I would try to maintain balance, even when under attack. I would work diligently to always right myself if ever I was found upon my back. I would not allow others to discourage me or my own thoughts to entomb me. I would not die in my shell! I would use my shell to my advantage, but it would not become my tomb!*

A pouch with a chisel caught my attention. What lesson could be contained within? By now much more time had passed than I had thought and though anxious to discover more simple truths, I returned the pouch to the trunk, looking forward to tomorrow.

SEARCHERS

The Chisel Pouch

The carpenter was well respected in the village. He always had time to listen. We were all amazed at his skill with the wood from which he shaped the necessities of our little village. Chairs and shelves were common. Wheels and tables, too! People far away, two and three days journey, knew of our carpenter! He was kind and good. His skill with wood was truly amazing. I asked him, "how do you carve a camel?" His animal carvings were truly life-like.

He replied, "I carve away the places that do not look like a camel." We laughed. He always made us happy.

I asked how he had acquired such skill. He told me that when he was very young he had learned by watching his father. He had watched and observed so much that when he was very young, he asked his father if he too could carve and build.

His father told him that before he could be a carpenter, he would have to discover the "secret" that allowed a carpenter to build, to carve, and to create.

"What is this great *secret* that a carpenter must learn, Master?"

He replied, "Watch the carpenter closely, Tadpole." I watched for many days.

"Do you now see what makes a carpenter great?" I answered by saying I had not yet discovered what makes a carpenter great. The Master suggested I ask the carpenter his secret.

So our most respected and loved village carpenter told me the *secret* that his father had told him. What made a carpenter great was really two things. The first was to be able to see the lion in the wood and the chair within the tree. The second was greater still. To see a lion in the wood meant nothing if it could not be removed. For this task a carpenter needed **TOOLS. TOOLS! Yes, the secret was before my eyes and I could not see! TOOLS to give shape and life to my ideas and dreams.**

Our village relied upon the carpenter very much. His goodness and kindness we enjoyed as much as his skills. I too began to desire the skill and to bring life from wood. My skills were improved because I respected my tools and I could see images in the trees. From time to time our village carpenter would show me ways to improve my skills and even make new tools for me. Our village carpenter so loved wood!

 What does this parable mean to you? Write briefly in the space below where you are now in your life with respect to the message of the parable.
_____
_____
_____
_____

TELESIS
IN SIGHT, IN MIND ™

As I held the carpenter's chisel in my hand and contemplated the parable I had just read, there came to my mind many thoughts. The carpenter's skill was determined by two great secrets! To remove a lion from the wood takes visualization and the proper tools.

This parable teaches that visualization of the end result is a necessary prerequisite to action. *You must be able to see what you hope to accomplish. Possessing the proper tools for the task provides for efficient effort.*

"So our most respected and loved village carpenter told me the *secret* that his father had told him. What made a carpenter great was really two things. The first was to be able to see the lion in the wood and the chair within the tree. The second was greater still. To see a lion in the woods meant nothing if it could not be removed. For this task a carpenter needed **TOOLS. TOOLS! Yes, the secret was before my eyes and I could not see! TOOLS to give shape and life to my ideas and dreams.**"

It is interesting to realize that the "searchers" of the past as well as those in the future will all face the same challenges and experiences to some degree. We are all faced with the same basic needs and wants. No wonder the wisdom of the parables are timeless. They are based upon our human nature. Times change, but human nature seems to remain constant. The same principles that assisted Thomas the seaman were the same ones that helped the Bedouin. William and Sarah applied the same principles in their lives. TOOLS then are the implements we use to move us forward. I should use education as a tool. Training as a tool. *Whatever moves me forward in helping me visualize my hopes and dreams are my tools.*

POUCHES

I determined after examining the chisel *that I would identify and sharpen my tools. For it is in them that lies the power to remove my hopes and dreams from this life's wood.* I could see in my mind the carpenter preparing for the days work by the way he respected his tools. The care with which he collected them at the end of the day and placed them safely away. I could also see the old Bedouin as he packed with care his belongings. Each item was important to his comfort and his survival. I could also see Thomas who learned how to tie proper knots as a seaman, and the various sundry articles he needed to be effective at his work. William and Sarah also experienced that there were no real short cuts to life. *They learned not only by their own experience, but also by seeking advice from others who were competent by their experience to give it to them. They also learned from the parables.*

The lobster, the turtle, and the carpenters chisel have revealed wisdom to me. I am pleased that *each of the "searchers" had felt an obligation to renew and pass on the wisdom of the parables.*

The sun has been up for some time now and I have other duties to do. However, I will reflect this day upon the carpenter and the importance of having the necessary tools for the task that comes before me. As I replaced the chisel pouch, the fish pouch captured my attention. Tomorrow it would teach me!

SEARCHERS

The Fish Pouch

 Master, how did you escape the fate of those who sit at the gates of the city, like that beggar over there who depends upon the charity of the stranger for his daily bread? Were you born of nobility and among the wealthy class?

"No, Tadpole. I was just as you are now. I was an orphan of the streets and also for a time I was at the mercy of the stranger for my daily bread."

How, Master, were you able to overcome this way of life and remove thyself from the bondage of poverty?

"My small friend and I depended upon each other for safety and we shared what we could gather. One day being very hungry we came upon a fisherman. He had caught but one fish. He turned to gather his net and my friend made good his escape with the fish. I was more fortunate than my friend for I was noticed and held tight by the fisherman."

How was this fortunate, Master? Surely you were punished for the fish was gone!

"It is as you say, Tadpole. I was taught to fish by this wise fisherman the rest of that afternoon until I had repaid seven fold his loss. At sunset this fisherman gave two of these fish to me and kept five for himself and his family."

But how does this explain how you overcome such poverty, Master?

"See the man in rags at the gates whose flesh hugs so tightly his bones? He is my childhood friend. *He has always traded what he wanted for the moment, for what he truly wanted.* He has always chosen the "fish" when opportunity came his way. It was the easy way and required no sacrifice. That afternoon so many years ago a wise fisherman knew if he taught me to fish he would not have to feed me each day, but I could feed myself for a lifetime."

But, Master, why did you not share your wealth with your childhood friend?

"Tadpole, **when a man receives alms without some effort or sacrifice required of him, he will eventually resent the giver, for he feels within himself that he is in bondage.** He has a resentment for me because I gave him fish. I should have taught him how to fish."

Master, how does one hold a net before casting it into the water? What time is best to fish? **TEACH ME TO FISH!**

 What does this parable mean to you? Write briefly in the space below where you are now in your life with respect to the message of the parable.
_____
_____
_____
_____

SEARCHERS

TELESIS
IN SIGHT, IN MIND ™

I had eagerly opened the trunk in anticipation of the contents of the pouch with the icon of the fish upon it. I determined it would be most beneficial for me to again review the parables I had read to this point. *No sooner did I see the emblems on the pouches than I began to see and visualize the story they represented.* Once I saw the image of the lobster, the parable came back to my mind without effort. The same experience came to me with each of the pouches I had opened and read. *There was something powerful about the association of the parable with the image/icon of the pouches.*

There was a great lesson for me to remember as well with the fish. To know how to fish was more important than to have a fish given to me. The philosophy of the "wants" I will emboss upon my mind. **"He has always traded what he wanted for the moment, for what he truly wanted."** I have made this mistake often in my life and from the wisdom of the fish parable it came to my realization with staggering force. *Often I had been the victim of my own lack of patience.* I wondered how many of the previous "searchers" experienced this same problem?

There was a second lesson in this simple parable. I had many times in my life hoped for the unearned and timely reward that I somehow expected might come to me. Surely I was worthy of good fortune! The fish taught me. **"When a man receives alms without some effort or sacrifice required of him, he will eventually resent the giver, for he feels within himself that he is in bondage."** I had not thought of the effects of the "unearned reward" this way or that it might have associated with it fetters and shackles and catch me unaware.

POUCHES

I have in my life experienced the affects of loaning money to someone and then noticing a change in our friendship. They felt a certain bondage to me because of the debt, just as I feel in bondage to those who have loaned me money. Truly, regardless of the time or the circumstance, most all of us have or will experience this. *I will pledge to myself to eventually live debt free and I will not trade what I may want at the moment for what I truly want.* Could these two jewels of wisdom have meant as much to the other "searchers?"

The contents of these pouches were having their accumulated affect upon me. *I began to sense a change in my basic ideas and assumptions about how life is to be experienced.* Could it be that I was becoming a "searcher" as well? Would there be some common bond that all who are searching experience? I looked at the remaining pouches within the trunk and speculated about the wisdom I would yet experience. Was I ready for them?

I began to consider the possible affect these simple pouches would have upon my future. There was certainly something soothing about these simple parables. *It is amazing how quickly time passes when we are involved with our emotions in something.* I was becoming very involved with the contents of this old trunk. My curiosity tempted me to hurriedly open each pouch and behold the contents. I felt a reluctance to yield. Their antiquity suggested an exercise in patience. Perhaps the turtle parable had already begun to have its affect upon me. *Be patient and be at peace* I thought to myself. There is time to savor each pouch and ponder what their contents mean to me! The cloud pouch looked interesting.

SEARCHERS

The Cloud Pouch

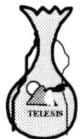 Master, why are we looking at the clouds? He replied, "When I desire to think and reason I often come to this mountain top and watch the clouds. They relax me and I feel at peace when I see them change shape and color." But Master, is this not a waste of time that could be better spent such as selling rugs in the market place? "I have lived many years, Tadpole, and have experienced much. You too can find peace in the clouds. To be so concerned with the market place can cause a man to bury his youth so far within himself that he forgets the simplest pleasures that brought so much peace and joy as a child."

But Master, I am anxious to begin my life and to acquire all the success that you have. How can I do this by watching the clouds? "Tadpole, I did not set out to acquire riches. It is true that I desired certain amounts of money to provide for my family, but this was not my heart's desire." What then, Master, has brought you all that you now possess?

"After many attempts at many things and many disappointments, **that which brought to me all that I have was courage, patience, imagination, and to see my future self** just as I can still see shapes in the clouds." I do not understand, Master. "Look at the clouds, Tadpole. What do you see? Look there and see the dove. Look there and behold the fox. Look there and notice the face of a beautiful maiden." Please, Master, explain more plainly to me that I might truly understand.

"**When I became aware that I should use my talents and do what interested me, this caused me much distress. I was comfortable**

POUCHES

before this restless feeling came upon me. It required courage for me to consider a change. I then had to be patient. As I came to this mountain to watch the clouds, I realized how many times the clouds changed to become something else. We change many times in our lives, Tadpole. **As we mature, as we experience, as we associate, we change**. Many feel these unsettling emotions and try to bury them. They should be recognized as opportunities to change and to experience new growth. When a man forgets the simple pleasures of his youth, when a man can no longer see shapes in the clouds, he has lost his ability to imagine, to contemplate, and to think of the possibilities. He must be able to see and to visualize his future self."

Master, my friends would laugh and think me a fool if I talked of these things.

"Riches come to a man when he decides to seek his heart's desire. **A heart's desire is true wealth,** Tadpole**. I determined to do what I enjoyed. Then the task was not work. I found I had more energy for that which interested me. This gave me confidence that my dreams would come to pass.** I forgot about trying to obtain riches. Instead I sought inner peace. To my surprise, riches began to find me."

Look, Master, in the clouds! There is a lion. Over there, see the serpent. There, there, see it! It is a chariot!

 What does this parable mean to you? Write briefly in the space below where you are now in your life with respect to the message of the parable.
_____
_____
_____
_____

SEARCHERS

TELESIS
IN SIGHT, IN MIND ™

Certainly it would be a great accomplishment to arrive at a state of peace and balance; to be relaxed with the way I live life. This parable of the clouds, why would "searchers" feel that it was significant enough to pass its wisdom on? And yet it reminds me of my own childhood. I often laid upon the grass as a child to contemplate the future. How often have I done that since those early years. I cannot remember how long ago it has been since I allowed myself this simple pleasure. I wondered if William and Sarah, after they read this parable, took the time to be together and contemplate their future possibilities. Perhaps they planned for their children, their work, or even their pleasures.

What about the old seaman, Thomas? Surely this parable would have extra significance for him. The clouds would tell an experienced seaman much about the weather. Would the seas be calm or churning? I imagined that Thomas would have thought much about the clouds in a given day. Maybe even the old Bedouin would have had the clouds as his companion as he tried to arrive at inner peace. The old "Master" had told tadpole he used the clouds to relax and find inner peace. *The clouds represented to the old "Master" that change comes many times to us as we go through life.*

Since I am now a fellow "searcher," I shall also remember the lesson in the clouds. "Riches come to a man when he decides to seek his heart's desire. **A heart's desire is true wealth,** Tadpole. **I determined to do what I enjoyed. Then the task was not work. I found I had more energy for that which interested me. This gave me confidence that my dreams would come to pass.** I forgot about trying to obtain riches. Instead I sought inner peace. To my surprise, riches began to find me."

POUCHES

I would do well to remember this in my search for life. I have always been aware of this way of thinking, but until lately, I thought they were too trivial, too simple, and too common in this day and age. I mean this is the nineties! I wonder if Thomas ever said that in his nineties. The eighteen nineties!

We, Tadpole and I, are not so different then. We each were burdened with the challenge of making our lives count for something. Who was this Tadpole of the parables? Who was the Master? I supposed I would find out as I read through the rest of the parables. I have to this point read five and there are eight left. What wisdom will they impart to me? Am I so different from Tadpole, the Bedouin, or Thomas, or William and Sarah? We could have lived at the same time and no doubt had much in common. *We all are trying to find our way through the wilderness of life. We are searching, to find out why we are here, where we came from, and where, when we are laid to rest, we might go.*

I determined to return the pouch of clouds to the trunk. It was time to go outside, lay upon the grass and look at the clouds. Perhaps they could help me think. I might even find peace in a busy day. Tomorrow I shall read from the pouch of money. I do not handle money well.

The Money Pouch

Master, I have learned much from the animals as I have observed them. Truly they have taught me many things. I have also learned much from our conversations. I desire to know something else, Master. I know you have become a successful man. I have heard of other successful men who acquired wealth such as you, but they have it no longer. How can I retain that which I earn and be wise with the wealth I gain? This is a question I wish you to answer.

"Tadpole, I will answer this question for I see by your asking it you have grown. I once heard of the richest man in Babylon who was to have practiced a wise principle. He believed and practiced that one tenth of all he earned was his to keep. I also practiced this principle. I have also been generous to those less fortunate than myself. **The greatest secret to managing wealth, however, is to know how money is tended. To this end I will explain.**

Money is like a flock of goats or sheep or any other animal. It takes a wise shepherd to care for his flocks. A man has one *she* goat and the man is hungry. Does he kill the goat or milk it? He is wise if he milks it, takes what he needs, then finds others who would buy or trade for his remainder. In a short passing of time, if he has been wise, he has enough goods or money to buy a *he* goat. Now the shepherd is ready to watch his flock multiply. He has offspring to sell, to eat or to barter for goods." Master, how should I be wise with money? I know how to milk a goat! Please explain further that I might understand.

"My young friend, do you not see or hear what I am telling you? Money is a flock just as are the shepherd's goats. **It is a wise shepherd who can give an accounting at the end of his day to determine from his numbers the safety of his flock.** He must keep his flock safe and attended lest some vanish in the night or fall prey to jackals. **Should not we all be shepherds over our flocks of money?** If a man has hundreds or thousands of goats and a jackal takes one of a hundred or a thousand it is not so serious a problem. But if a man has only ten or even three and loses one this is a great loss. To those who have but few goats or little money it is most important that they are the most diligent in making a daily accounting.

The secret with which I have retained my wealth is **I have always known how much money I have had at any time of the day.** This helps me to plan. It relieves me of many burdens. **My wife and children also practice this secret. They are accountable for their flocks of money. My entire family knows that money can provide freedom or bondage.**

When seven days have come and gone four times we discuss and report how wise or foolish we have been with money. Those who have been the most foolish of my children have been those who did not record what they spent. **To those of my children who have recorded their purchases and been wise about the use of money I have given them more**. I gave all my children three coins each. Now some have none, some only three, some many more, even one has twenty pieces of silver and two of gold." I see, Master, what you are telling me is true. I have seen it in our village. **Those who know how to manage their money seem to have a happier life.**

"Young friend, **the lack of money makes all other problems seem bigger than they really are. I have seen my friends over the years become victims and in bondage because they did not know that to retain their money, they must care for it just as they do a flock of goats. To be responsible and wise with money you must know what you have, where it is spent, how much you can reasonably**

expect tomorrow, and the next day. Above all you must record daily what happens to money.

If you practice this great secret you will in time be free of debt, out of bondage, able to do much good, and be free. Yet my friend there is also another great secret about money. Like a goat, money can also have offspring. The offspring of money is called USURY.

 What does this parable mean to you? Write briefly in the space below where you are now in your life with respect to the message of the parable.
_____
_____
_____
_____

POUCHES

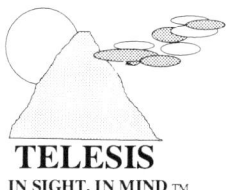

TELESIS
IN SIGHT, IN MIND ™

If I needed good advice with money this was it. I had heard most of this before but it had not been presented to me in this simple way. It really is important to realize that money can have "progeny." The progeny or offspring of money is usury/interest. The trouble is that we usually pay interest creating progeny for someone else and usually that is the bank or creditor.

I reasoned that perhaps William and Sarah had concerns about this as well. After all they were retiring from the freight business and all of their children were doing well. I wondered if these simple rules of finance were the reason for their success in money management. *It would be nice to control money rather than be controlled by it.* This then would become my challenge. Challenge is the correct word because *it would be difficult at first to change my old habits* and perspective about the use or misuse of my money.

The old Master from the parable said, "**The greatest secret to managing wealth, however, is to know how money is tended.**" To be a shepherd over our flocks of money is a challenge. What else was it he told the younger man. "**It is a wise shepherd who can give an accounting at the end of his day to determine from his numbers the safety of his flock.**" I could certainly do better in my record keeping. He mentioned a daily accounting as opposed to weekly or monthly. This would seem like sound advice. I guess the reasoning behind this is that *if a shepherd is missing a sheep it would be easier to find if it had only been missing a day than to discover it had been missing a week or a month.* The practice of allowing others in the family to know the situation might just also teach them restraint in its use. After all *it is difficult to change a behavior* like spending money if one is not aware of how money may provide freedom or bondage.

People are not that different today. We all eventually discover that the value of money changes constantly every day of our lives. I mean by this that the value of a dollar seems greater somehow when there is less in ones possession. If I have one thousand dollars a single dollar seems to have less value than if I have only two dollars. Truly the parable is correct when it says that, **the lack of money makes all other problems seem bigger than they really are.** I have dealt with the frustration of having a limited source of money when time and circumstance dictated and required more of it than I had.

Certainly the wisdom of this parable is worth remembering. "**I have seen my friends over the years become victims and in bondage because they did not know that to retain their money, they must care for it just as they do a flock of goats. To be responsible and wise with money you must know what you have, where it is spent, how much you can reasonably expect tomorrow, and the next day. Above all you must record daily what happens to money.** If you practice this great secret you will in time be free of debt, out of bondage, able to do much good, and be free." I see the wisdom in this simple parable and because of this I resolved to live debt free and release myself from bondage.

I have learned from the pouches a great deal. Could they also teach me how to improve my skills when dealing with people? We all have to deal with others whatever we do for our daily bread. I returned the money pouch to the trunk. The wheel pouch with its many spokes, I chose as my next lesson.

POUCHES

The Wheel Pouch

What is it, Master, that seems to command the respect that others have for you? Is it money? "To some it may seem my wealth is the reason I have gained a certain amount of respect. However, **I prefer to believe that respect comes to the person who is tolerant of others imperfections!** I have tried since early in my life to allow others their imperfections. Consider the wheel, my young friend. What is there about a wheel that can teach you how to treat people?"

Master, I do not know how a wheel can teach me about people. Please, tell me how a wheel has within itself such knowledge! "Remember the Lobster? Because you were able to **see beyond the limits of your eyes** you obtained knowledge. Now, go and observe the wheel. When you feel you have gained knowledge, return and tell me what you have learned from the wheel."

And so I observed the wheel with the perspective of how it could teach me about people. Since I had been taught by the Master to observe not only the lobster, but also the turtle, and the clouds I felt better prepared to learn from the wheel. So I endeavored once again to see beyond the sight of my eyes. I continued to ponder and reason the knowledge of the wheel into the afternoon. By the setting of the sun I was still unable to understand. My eyes grew heavy some time into the night and while in my slumber **when my mind was at peace I began to see beyond the limits of my sight**. As I saw I considered the wheel. The wheel began to reveal its knowledge. The wheel receives its **purpose from its shape**. Its **spokes lend it strength.** The faster **the wheel spins** the more resistant it is to change its direction, **preserving its balance**. I pondered the wheel. How is this knowledge within the wheel to help me when I associate with people? Of all the shapes the

SEARCHERS

wheel is most efficient to move or carry a load. Consider the square. It is a wheel with the edges removed. I should see people as wheels, not hard edges of a square and with imperfections. **Each person through use and time is made more efficient for the loads of life.** I should be patient and allow each person their imperfections until time and experience has smoothed their edges. When you are asked to manage people one must remember the spokes. **Strength comes from different directions and all spokes meet at the center of the wheel.** When dealing with people I should remember the spokes and realize that different people are going to come from different directions when determining solutions to a problem. I should allow others to solve the task from their direction. **All spokes find their way to the center. They simply come from different directions, and this lends strength to the wheel.** When a wheel has motion, it becomes resistant to any change in direction. Consider a man or woman. Balance is maintained when they have direction, and they are in motion. The faster the wheel spins the more difficult it is to upset its direction. **I should allow people to have a purpose and give them freedom in direction. This empowers them with motion giving them ability to maintain balance while moving forward.** Yes, this is the knowledge of the wheel.

Master, the wheel has revealed unto me its knowledge. "It is well that you have learned respect can be achieved by allowing others to learn by experience. It takes patience to be tolerant, Tadpole. Yes, you learned this lesson well."

What does this parable mean to you? Write briefly in the space below where you are now in your life with respect to the message of the parable.
_____
_____
_____
_____

TELESIS
IN SIGHT, IN MIND ™

Who would have thought that a wheel could represent the way we should interact with those with whom we associate! The interaction of people has been the same through the centuries I suppose. How much money has been lost or gained strictly on the basis of the way a situation unfolded over moments? *Respect earned by the tolerance we accept of others imperfections could go a long way to building relationships.* After all it is relationships that prove to be our undoing or our success.

So now I have the wheel in my hands contemplating the simple truths about human interaction. Be tolerant of others imperfections. *It is true that we are all different and we approach life and all of our specific situations from different directions just as the spokes of the wheel approach the hub.* Surely then the strength derived from such an arrangement is worth thinking about. I have been the victim of those persons who dictate policy and methodology expecting it to be done their way as if there could be no better approach to the problem.

The very symmetry of a wheel signifies balance and organization. But again the same symmetry and organization is represented best from the many directions of its spokes. I will never look at a wheel again in the same way. Now whenever I see a wheel it will remind me to be tolerate of others imperfections. We are all different and this brings strength to any hub or center. I will apply this simple knowledge in my own life or pursuits. Surely my interactions with people will then be more worthwhile and at the same most likely more rewarding. *If respect can be had it will come naturally to one who is genuinely tolerant of others imperfections.*

SEARCHERS

I would imagine the old seaman was reminded of this fact every moment he steered his ship. For the sailing ship had for its helm a spoked wheel! Surely Thomas was aware of this parable and ran an efficient ship because of his knowledge of the wheel. When he may have forgotten the wheels wisdom it would not have been for long. No ship or captain could stay on course whose hands never came back to the wheel.

What of William and Sarah? Likewise the wheel parable must have a special significance for them. Being in the freight business early this century with horse drawn wagons, the spoked wheel would be everywhere. How could they escape the wisdom of the wheel once they had read the parable. They could not! The way they interacted with people must have been influenced by the knowledge of the wheel!

It would seem wise to not only learn from the wheel but to also in some ways try to be like the wheel. **"When a wheel has motion, it becomes resistant to any change in direction. Consider a man or woman. Balance is maintained when they have direction, and they are in motion. The faster the wheel spins the more difficult it is to upset its direction."**

I looked at the old trunk and wondered about those people who had it in their possession but never discovered the wealth of wisdom it contained. They could have become "searchers" as well. They dared not dream! *Is that the key to becoming a "searcher," to dare to dream?* I wished I could have seen all those who came so close to having the contents of this old trunk revealed. I closed the trunk with the thought, how has or will my life be changed because I was "searching," dared to dream, and opened what others, except for other "searchers," saw as an old empty trunk! I knew I would learn again. The pouch of a rising sun held promise.

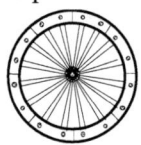

POUCHES

The Sun Pouch

 Good morning, Master. The sun begins to rise in the east. It is early and the birds have only been about their singing for a short time. Master, may I ask that you teach me more? I have come to realize I am ill prepared in many ways to move ahead.

"Yes, it is a morning to make one give thanks and to be reverent for his life. **The morning is a powerful time of day, my young friend. It is the birthing of a new day.** The sun rising in the east can inspire many ideas. What is it that you wish to know?" I desire to know how you have become so confident that all will be well. You do not ever seem to be troubled or worried. How have you attained such peace? "I have my troubles and worries like any other man. I have peace because **the sun comes up**." Master, I have come to know well **the method by which you teach me.** I will watch the rising of the sun and then I will report to you in three days my thoughts and observations about the sun.

I watched the sun rise each day in the east. **The sun gives notice each day before it is seen.** The darkness flees before its presence. Between its rising and setting all life experiences change. The changes and events of the day are varied and different for each form of life. There is great complexity throughout a day. **All forms of life are interwoven like some great spider web.** Yet, through all this change remains one great constant, **the sun comes up**. Everything depends upon the sun. Light and warmth is given freely to all. The chill of the night can be tolerated because the sun comes up. Flowers withhold their opening. The birds withhold their singing until they rejoice at first light in the knowledge that **the sun comes up**. I came to know everyone needs to believe that there is something we can look to as unchanging, ever constant, and always certain. Something even more

39

powerful than a mother's love. I wonder, is there such a thing so powerful?

"Ah, my young friend, I see that you are up early again this morning. I have seen you at a distance each day as you have watched the rising of the sun upon the crest of the hill. **I too have watched from there. It is a special place. What have you come to understand from the sun? Have you learned or discovered a path upon which to place your feet?**"

It would seem to me, Master, that you have come to realize through your life a certain philosophy to deal with changing events. Is this not so? "Yes, it is as you suppose. Like the sun I have tried to remain constant in a changing world. The sun is above all things. **The world turns below and there is not anything that is not observed by the sun. Nothing goes unnoticed.** I have determined that in my own world, my life, its daily events shall not pass unnoticed. When unexpected trials and challenges have come to me I have remembered, as I have suffered in them, that they will pass. When I have had much success and have been the most joyful, I have also tried to remain humble because I know that it will also pass. **Some circumstances come, only to pass.** But in their coming I have gained experience. When life's challenges come to me, no matter the circumstance, I have tried to remember **the sun comes up**."

What does this parable mean to you? Write briefly in the space below where you are now in your life with respect to the message of the parable.

_____
_____
_____
_____

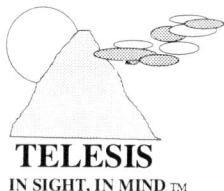

TELESIS
IN SIGHT, IN MIND ™

It was morning when I returned to the trunk. The sun was coming in the window at a low angle but with definite authority. Birds were greeting the sun with a friendly mixture of sounds. The early morning rays of light rested peacefully upon the old trunk as if they were old friends. It seemed fitting somehow that I had determined previously to read from the sun pouch this morning. I raised the lid and reached for the sun and read the parable.

They are right, the Master and Tadpole, the morning truly is a powerful time of the day. I imagined how beautiful the rising and the setting of the sun on the oceans would be. Thomas, the seaman, must have enjoyed the beginning and ending moments of the day.

I hadn't thought much of the notion about how *everything is interwoven like some great spider web.* It seems in this day and age we look to monitors such as computers and TV for our enjoyment. How many of us take the time to be alone long enough, and early enough to watch the most constant thing in our lives announce its presence. The sun truly is the one great constant in our lives. We can look to the sun for peace, security, and take comfort that the world will have light. We can exercise faith in the sun. So many things seem to destroy our faith these days. But in the sun we have constancy in ever changing times.

As I read the parable of the sun I seemed to be whisked away and found myself present on the hill with the Master and his pupil. I could hear the lesson being taught and enjoyed the moment with them as the sun came up. I must have been totally engrossed in my thoughts and the visualizations that were coming to mind, for when I seemed to be brought back to the present moment by some movement or sound, I noticed that the sun had continued its rising and now its rays of light were illuminating the trunk in different places. I was impressed that perhaps almost an hour had passed while I had been pondering the parable of the sun. *It is amazing how much concentration we can give something or someone when that something or someone has our present interest.*

I thought how correct their assumption was that everything is so dependent upon the sun. Yet we accept the sun's presence with such a common complacency that it comes and goes almost without notice, unless we plan an outing. We complain if it's too hot, or if it's not warm enough. How would we react if tomorrow the sun never came up?

The lesson here seems to be to reverence the sun. *Be grateful for another day of life and take comfort in the knowledge that the sun does come up offering us a chance to improve our efforts over and above those of yesterday. Be confident that whatever is causing us problems for the moment will eventually pass.*

I have learned that there are at least two great constants in the world. **Things always change**, and always **the sun comes up**! When I become discouraged I will observe the rising of the sun and share the experience with a friend.

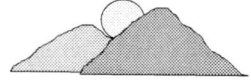

POUCHES

The Friend Pouch

 Master, you have taught me many things that have been of great worth to me. I have learned much and will strive to remember the lessons I have been taught. I feel of late a certain desire to share what I have learned with someone else.

"Ah yes, my young friend, you have come to know the value of truth. **Truth is something that is independent of its source. Wherever you see it, you should embrace it.** When you have benefited from it sufficiently to understand what you have received, it is most appropriate to share it with someone. But, you must be careful with whom you share such knowledge. When the time is right you will know, within yourself, and recognize the one who is to receive what you have come to know."

Why is it important that I be so careful to whom I teach and share my ideas?

"Ideas are very fragile when they are first conceived. They should be exposed only to those whom we can trust and that we know will encourage us. Some knowledge is for the world. Some is reserved for those with whom we have a special bond or friendship. There can be an increased power associated with someone you can trust. I have been most fortunate to have many such friends. **For me I consider my wife my best friend.** We can talk and visit about everything. We enjoy each other's company and prefer it to any others. There are also others from whom we receive strength, and to whom we might strengthen. Some day you too will find such a friend."

SEARCHERS

Until such time, Master, how shall I teach what I have come to know. It fills me with a great desire to share with others.

"At the correct moment you will become aware that someone must know what you know. **At such a time you will feel within yourself that truth must pass between you.** The power of this experience is, that by sharing, you will also be taught some truth you had not known before. This is the great value in having a friend."

What makes a friend so worth having, Master?

"When you are struggling with your ideas, true friends give you encouragement. When you are trying to move forward they will assist you without feeling threatened, and despite your weaknesses they will remind you of your strengths. If you desire a happy life seek out and associate with people who will make true friends."

How do I meet and make such friends, Master?

"Life will bring these people to you. By sharing truth with them you will become friends."

 What does this parable mean to you? Write briefly in the space below where you are now in your life with respect to the message of the parable.

_____
_____
_____
_____

POUCHES

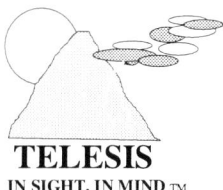

TELESIS
IN SIGHT, IN MIND ™

It had been nine days since I had acquired the trunk and I had learned much and thought a great deal about the things I had learned. I was eager to begin the next adventure into the trunk. Funny, I had an urge to be up early this morning and I watched the sun rise. It had been years since I have done that. It felt good to have a head start on the neighborhood. I thought it would be nice to share the morning with a friend as the sun came up.

The pouch that I reached for had two hands clasping. I unrolled the linen inside and read the parable from the penned hand of Sarah who had rewritten it to preserve it. I felt a certain friendship with my fellow "searchers" convinced I would have enjoyed their company.

I have many friends in the simplest definition of the word, but the word friend seems to go to a much greater depth with some of my friends. This is what the parable of the friend seems to be about. The depth of friendship can take us to heights we may not achieve entiely on our own.

I know what it feels like to have ideas belittled or dismissed without consideration. *Ideas are fragile and they should only be shared with confidence to those we know with depth assisting us to greater heights.* Our best friend is someone we trust. I am sure that William and Sarah were the best of friends. Certainly "searchers," when they know each other, have a common bond much stronger than most.

The great lesson here is the knowledge that **"Life will bring these people to you. By sharing truth with them you will become friends."** "*At the correct moment you will become aware that someone must know what you know.* **At such a time you will feel**

45

within yourself that truth must pass between you. The power of this experience is, that by sharing, you will also be taught some truth you had not known before. This is the great value in having a friend."

Having read the parable, I determined to be more appreciative of my friends. I realized that of all the fates that can come to a man or woman, the saddest is having no one to call friend. It is a great thing to have a friend you can share truth with, and despite the truth, you know your friendship will stand.

It was becoming obvious to me, that the wealth of this old trunk was indeed of greater value than I had supposed. I was beginning to feel a certain regret because I could see that only four pouches remained. There must have been more at some time. Were there only thirteen? I looked at the remaining pouches and saw the eagle, the eye, the sea wave, and the chest. Though it had not seemed that there was a specific order with which to read from the pouches, I felt within me that I was to read the chest pouch last of all. It was only the feeling, nothing else, that suggested this to me. The time I had allowed myself to study from the trunk was gone and I had to be about my day. However, I had learned to appreciate my friends. I was determined to share some truth with a special friend, when life revealed this person to me. What better symbol than a small brass ring to symbolize friendship. Was it one of Sarah's?

POUCHES

The Eagle Pouch

Good morning, Master. It is as you have said. The morning is a powerful time of the day. Since I have learned that **the sun comes up,** I have faced each day since with greater peace. I also have met a friend.

"It is fitting that you have enjoyed the power of an early rising from your bed. It clears the mind and you become aware of all that is living. I am pleased that life has brought you a friend. You must be anxious to share some truth and knowledge. Is this not so?"

Yes it is, Master. I do desire to share what I have discovered. I am very anxious to begin experimenting with my ideas. I have prepared as best I can. **Master, when do I know that the time for preparation is over and the time to begin is at hand?**

"Tadpole, I have noticed not far from here an eagle's nest. For weeks an eagle pair have cared for their young. Of the three, only one remains. I have watched them closely since hatching. One fell to earth to its death because it tried to leave the nest not having exercised or tested its wings against the wind. The second, feeling sorry for itself refused food and instruction when offered, then died. **The third I have watched with interest because it seems to know by instinct what to do and when to do it.** I wish to be present when it realizes it must leave the safety of its nest before it can find the freedom that awaits before it can soar to new heights. Come, Tadpole, we shall go as you have done before and together we shall discover the answer to your question."

SEARCHERS

I see, Master, that the young eagle is fully feathered. He stands at the edge and tests his wings, but his feet are firmly planted in the nest. See, he is beckoned aloft by others of his kind.

"You are about to witness a great event in the life of an eagle, Tadpole, the time when it discovers the purpose of its wings. Notice that it has moved from the center of the nest to its edge. I feel we are only moments away from the greatest event in the eagle's life. **The moment it realizes that in order for it to fly it must place itself at risk and rely upon its weeks of exercise and preparation."**

Master, do you suppose the young eagle is afraid? "The extent to which it might fear would no doubt be dependent upon the confidence it has in its preparation. **The young eagle knows within itself when the time is right. It relies upon instinct, an inner power, to overcome the caution it must feel."**

Master, I have learned I am as this young eagle. I have prepared, but feel a certain caution that a little more preparation is best advised. Is this not wise before I test my ideas? "There is a time for flapping wings and a time for using them. Look, Tadpole! He placed faith in his wings, jumped free and now he soars! Listen to his joyful call of triumph! **Do the thing which you fear and the death of that fear will be certain."**

What does this parable mean to you? Write briefly in the space below where you are now in your life with respect to the message of the parable.

TELESIS
IN SIGHT, IN MIND ™

It is day ten since I acquired the trunk or was it a chest that I should call it now. Since I have a fondness for the out-of-doors I reached for the eagle pouch with anticipation for the simple story that I knew would have significant wisdom. It seemed I had much in common with the young pupil of the Master, who he referred to as Tadpole. Why was he called Tadpole, surely he had a name? Anyway, I began to read and it was early in the morning. The sun parable was more powerful than I had thought. The question that Tadpole asked the Master about preparation came to my mind with real force. How many times had I asked myself this same question? **Master, when do I know that the time for preparation is over and the time to begin is at hand?**

In my life I could see that I had been similar to each of the young eagles at different times. *Sometimes I have tried to move too suddenly for the task, being ill prepared and failed. Other times I have refused instruction and had to suffer the consequences, and the best of times have been when I had the courage to take action.*

Again I found myself mentally with the Master and Tadpole and listening to them talk of the eagle. I could see in my mind again all that was transpiring as the young eagle soared. I could almost hear the joyful and confident celebrating call of that young eagle myself.

I felt a certain relief in knowing that I have not been alone with the feelings of self doubt and uncertainty. These feelings are normal and seem to be experienced by all at some time. I thought it interesting that William and Sarah placed within this pouch an eagle feather. They probably wore the one out that Thomas placed in the pouch for them.

They probably stroked it many times as they reviewed this parable of the eagle, just as I find myself stroking this one, the one they placed in the pouch for me.

Thomas, being so much at sea, must have had a greater appreciation for the albatross than he would have the eagle. The sea birds must have been an important part of Thomas' day. The gull and the albatross certainly would have reminded him of the eagle.

I read again from the parable because it was something that Tadpole said to the Master that I could relate to with haunting familiarity. He said, "Master, I have learned I am as this young eagle. I have prepared, but feel a certain caution that a little more preparation is best advised. Is this not wise before I test my ideas?" I have felt this same caution. The Master gave the answer when he said, "There is a time for flapping wings and a time for using them. Look, Tadpole! He placed faith in his wings, jumped free and now he soars! Listen to his joyful call of triumph! **Do the thing which you fear and the death of that fear will be certain.**"

What timely advice for me at this junction in my life. Why have I been so fortunate to have the chest in my possession? Why did I have the dream? What is the significance of the emblem that is the same on each pouch? Perhaps these answers are yet to come. There are three pouches left to open.

POUCHES

The Eye Pouch

Master, you have a reverence for all that is in this world. I have never met anyone so aware of his surroundings. You seem to notice everything and appreciate its existence. How did you come to reverence these things?

"This characteristic often comes quite naturally **when you begin to see things as they really are. Two things must always be considered. They are time and distance.** I will explain. If I wish to observe an ant, it is best observed during the daylight. You must also be very close to it. If I wish to observe the hills and valleys, this is best done from a mountain top. Time and distance are important when one wishes to learn by observation."

I understand, Master. Had we not been at the proper distance, and at the appropriate time, we would not have observed the young eagle leave its nest.

"Sometimes, Tadpole, **our minds do not correctly identify what our eye actually sees.** A branch may be perceived as a snake. We must be on guard that we do not deceive ourselves. **We must learn to apply a proper use of distance at the correct time when we are trying to solve a problem."**

Master, will you explain further that I may more fully understand.

"As you wish. Hold this coin close to your eye. It is possible to hide even the sun from view. But the use of the coin in this manner will not allow you to see the correct path that may lead to a far horizon. You see, the proper use of distance at the right time, can be very

51

powerful. **You must be able to see at many depths and distances, Tadpole."**

But, Master, I see how this will help me as I travel. Will this knowledge also help to deal with people?

"Ah, Tadpole, it pleases me that you ask this question. **The greatest challenge is to reverence man. So often man deserves it the least and needs it the most.** It is a great talent to possess. By this I mean, **we must be willing to see each individual at any depth of their soul or personality. We must be willing to allow them their imperfections. We must be willing and able to see people in depth at any distance at any time**. Cultivate this ability, Tadpole, and it will serve you well.

I see the wisdom in the things you have told me, Master. There is so much to learn! How shall I ever be prepared for life?

"You may not always be prepared, Tadpole, but you can always determine which path to choose in a given situation. This will allow you to maintain poise and balance when you are surprised or caught off guard. Remember, Tadpole, to maintain a proper distance at any given time. **The eye can often be easily deceived.**

What does this parable mean to you? Write briefly in the space below where you are now in your life with respect to the message of the parable.

_____
_____
_____

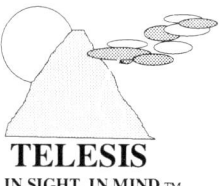

TELESIS
IN SIGHT, IN MIND ™

Although the sun parable and the friend parable seemed to teach some principles of common sense and tolerance when dealing with people, and to emphasize the importance of rising early and looking forward to the future, the parable of the eye caused me to think about how I see or do not see my surroundings. The Master had a reverence for all things animate or inanimate. It was this respect for all things that brought him a certain inner peace. Even from the beginning in the lobster parable, the Master emphasized this when he said, "You must learn to see beyond the sight of your own eye." There is much more going on around us at any time than we realize.

The eye as the symbol of this parable seemed appropriate enough. I have been fooled many times by my eye. Many situations and circumstances, after the passing of time, were often much different than what I thought I had seen. What was it the Master said? "This characteristic often comes quite naturally **when you begin to see things as they really are. Two things must always be considered. They are time and distance.** I will explain. If I wish to observe an ant, it is best observed during the daylight. You must also be very close to it. If I wish to observe the hills and valleys, this is best done from a mountain top. Time and distance are important when one wishes to learn by observation."

It would seem from the parable that it is necessary to observe from the correct perspective. Since *the elapse of time, the angle, and the distance from what is being observed is critical to accuracy.* I must remember to avoid hearsay or speculation. I will have many decisions to make in life and *I can ill afford to base decisions on inaccurate or distorted information about people or circumstance.*

SEARCHERS

How many times have I missed opportunity because I may have made my decisions on inaccurate assessment, faulty assumption, and a shallow depth of focus? It is probably best not to know. Yet, by knowing, perhaps I could avoid a repeat of my folly. Why is it that we seem to jump to conclusions? I suppose because it requires less effort than learning how to properly observe.

There will be many people I will have to deal with in my life. I will have to rely upon my personal skills of interaction to be successful. It will be wise for me to remember the Master's council. "**The greatest challenge is to reverence man. So often man deserves it the least and needs it the most.** It is a great talent to possess. By this I mean, **we must be willing to see each individual at any depth of soul or personality. We must be willing to allow their imperfections. We must be willing and able to see people in depth at any distance at any time**. Cultivate this ability, Tadpole, and it will serve you well."

I was starting to feel like Tadpole. He had said to the Master, There is so much to learn! How shall I ever be prepared for life? **"You may not always be prepared, Tadpole, but you can always determine which path to choose in a given situation.** This will allow you to maintain poise and balance when you are surprised or caught off guard. Remember, Tadpole, to maintain a proper distance at any given time. **The eye can often be easily deceived."**

Well, there is wisdom here, and I would make every effort to apply it from now on.

POUCHES

The Sea Pouch

Master, the wind blows. It comes fresh from the sea and the waves are gentle mounds. I have been frightened by the sea. The sea is enjoyable to watch, but I struggle, and I do not feel comfortable when I am within it.

"My young friend, what has caused this feeling within you about the sea? I sense a certain foreboding that is not your usual self. Do you wish to share your feelings with me? I am here for you if you wish to talk."

The sea is not supportive, Master. It is difficult to rise high enough in the water, with waves about, to see very far. Many times I have become frightened because I have not been able to see the shore. **When I cannot see the shore, I do not know which way to swim.**

"When is it that you are at peace with the sea, Tadpole?" I am at peace when I see the shore and I know in which direction to swim. "Where do you go to find peace, to think, or to dream? Do you have such a place, Tadpole? If not, I suggest that you find one. We must sometimes be alone to be at peace. Sometimes we can only be at peace when we are with others. **Inner peace comes to us when we have dreams of hope.**" Do you fear the sea, Master? Does it cause you concern? How are you at peace with the sea?

"There have been times when I was afraid of the sea. **My fear was born of misunderstanding and a lack of knowledge of the unknown.** It is true that one can be within the sea, but one can also be upon it! Unlike earth, you cannot leave footprints in the sea.

However, the sea has certain secrets it reveals to those who wish to understand. **To be at peace with the sea is to understand it."** Life is as a sea. Is this not true, Master?

"Yes, I have found this to be so. We can choose to be within it, or we can choose to rise above it." We sink or swim in life because of the choices we make. **Each decision moves us away from some choices and toward other choices. This is important to remember. When we have the opportunity to do so, we should take advantage and ride the crest of the wave, for this wave will usually take us to shore."**

Master, how does one make the correct choices? The ability to choose wisely would be of great value to me. "Experience will make you wise, Tadpole, but keep in mind that **decisions are made much easier when you can see a shore upon which to plant your feet.** Remember that tracks are not left in the sea, but they can be left upon the shore. **You must understand life to rise above it,** Tadpole!"

What does this parable mean to you? Write briefly in the space below where you are now in your life with respect to the message of the parable.

_____
_____
_____
_____

POUCHES

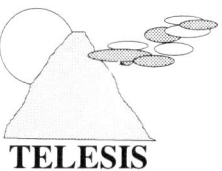

TELESIS
IN SIGHT, IN MIND ™

The eye parable was still on my mind. So often in the past I have made mistakes I could easily have avoided, if I had only been taught, or by instinct, been aware of its simple wisdom. I was becoming aware of a progression within the parables, at least within the order I had dealt with them. The first five seemed to focus more upon the principles I needed to apply to myself. These principles being how to deal with change, patience, tolerance, proper knowledge, and imagining the success I might seek. Then there was the money parable! This simple lesson in personal finance if properly practiced, could keep me out of bondage and living free. The lessons of the wheel, the sun, and who could forget the importance of good friends and associations seemed important for interaction. The eagle parable so visually explained that there is a proper time to move ahead and take the risk, after the necessary preparation has been exercised. There were just two pouches left. The sea pouch and the chest pouch.

I placed the shell in front of me before I began to read. I thought it might be worth a few moments of time to reflect upon all that had come to me in these simple pouches. This reflection seemed to put my mind in tune.

There was some great symbolism here. Life, as Tadpole observed, really is as the sea. Our challenge *is* to sink within it or to rise above it! I have not been on the sea often, but on those occasions that I have, it has been a powerful experience. It is so vast that I felt very small.

I was concluding that if we fear the sea or life, it is mostly because we usually lack knowledge or direction. *We usually fear something because we do not understand it.* Understanding brings with it as its companion, inner peace. There have been times when I have been up to my ears in life struggling for breath and seeking a shore to swim toward. Other times I have had the faith as it were, to rise up, and walk on the top of life, because I found direction.

I closed my eyes, placed the shell near my ear, and listened to the sea. **"To be at peace with the sea is to understand it."** Life is as a sea. Is this not true, Master? The words of the parable came to me again.

I continued to listen. "Yes, I have found this to be so. We can choose to be within it, or we can choose to rise above it." *We sink or swim in life because of the choices we make.* **Each decision moves us away from some choices and toward other choices. This is important to remember. When we have the opportunity to do so, we should take advantage and ride the crest of the wave, for this wave will usually take us to shore."**

It had been twelve days that I had the chest and studied its contents. The final pouch was before me. Tomorrow I would open it. I still had the shell to my ear and while looking at the chest pouch the final words of the sea parable echoed in my ear. **"You must understand life to rise above it,** Tadpole!"

POUCHES

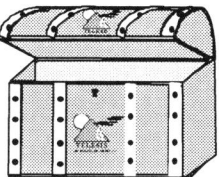

The Chest Pouch

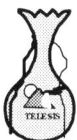 Master, we have met often and discussed many things. I have learned much. It has been a most interesting time. I feel confident that I can move forward with life. I thank you for your patience.

"Tadpole, it has brought me much happiness and joy to watch you gain knowledge and wisdom. You have indeed learned many things. **I have observed your thirst for knowledge and your desire to participate in life. Many people are mere spectators.** It is time that I show you my greatest treasure. Would you like to see it?" Oh yes, Master! To see what you, a very wealthy man, considers his greatest treasure has been a great curiosity of mine. I would be honored to see such a priceless jewel. "Perhaps you shall be disappointed, Tadpole, It may not be what you expect. You have lived with an image in your mind of what you suppose my greatest treasure is like. You suspect great jewels! **My treasure is far greater than jewels.** Come, we shall go to my home."

Master, how many servants guard this treasure? Surely it must require many to keep it safe!

"I have no one to guard it, but it is always safe. I have shown it to many, but they do not understand its worth. I have allowed many to see, handle, and examine my jewels but they are always disappointed and think me a fool. Perhaps you shall also, Tadpole. Now, go to the chest near the wall and satisfy the curiosity and mental image you expect my treasure to be."

SEARCHERS

Oh, Master! Indeed it is not what I imagined at all. I finally understand all that you have been so patiently trying to teach me. These things are truly responsible for all your wealth, aren't they? I see why others would think you are a fool! "Tadpole, the contents before you have been my greatest treasures. **I only have to see them regularly** and hold them. **My mind recalls and presents to me what they mean and what they inspire within me.** These were the objects that an old friend so long ago used to teach me as I have tried to teach you."

This sea shell, Master, reminds me of the **lobster**. This square and chisel, the story of the **carpenter**. When I see this piece of net, I think of the **fish** and the beggar boy. Oh, Master, even a **turtle** shell! An old **eagle** feather, a small **spoked wheel**, and a carving of **clasping hands**. **What do all these other objects represent, Master?** I see that there is so much you haven't taught me.

Master, "Yes, Tadpole." What is your name? "My name is Τελεσισ." What does your name mean, Master? "It is from the Greeks, Tadpole, it means *fulfillment*." I wish I had such a grand name, Master, but I am an orphan of the streets. "Tadpole, I shall call you Ανακρινο a *"searcher."* For you have sought wisdom. I wish to give you this. Wear it as a daily reminder of the things which you have come to know. When your life draws near its end as mine is now, pass it to the next "searcher." At my passing the chest shall be yours."

 What does this parable mean to you? Write briefly in the space below where you are now in your life with respect to the message of the parable.

_____
_____
_____
_____

POUCHES

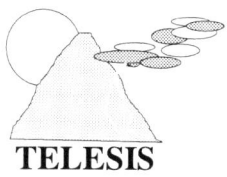

TELESIS
IN SIGHT, IN MIND ™

 I was up early and eager to open the last pouch. The chest pouch had been on my mind for days. I had the impression days ago that I should save it for the last. The sun was coming up. It was the birthing of a new day and I was ready. The lid of the chest came up with ease. The pouches were just as I had lain them. The chest pouch! Finally I would learn from it! What would be inside? The leather of the pouch was soft and supple. No doubt somewhat preserved from the natural oils from the hands of "searchers" who had handled it so many times. I pulled the draw strings and emptied the contents into my hand. There it was before me. Of course, it was so obvious that I wondered why I had not thought of it. It was the *emblem* on the ring, Ανακρινο's ring, or more accurately the ring of Τελεσισ, that was the jewel. The ring would be an ever present reminder. All that I had learned would come to my sight and into my mind as long as I wore the ring of Τελεσισ. It would constantly remind me to review the parables of Τελεσισ. The linen upon which this parable had been written, and the ring were not the pouches only contents. There was also an old animal skin. At the top was the emblem and a written message. It read:

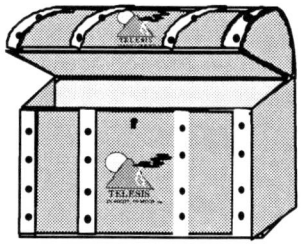

TELESIS
IN SIGHT, IN MIND ™

My name is Anakrino, the "searcher." My friend TELESIS taught me about life from the simple objects from his chest. I, too, was an orphan in our village and grew up without a name. TELESIS had risen above the same fate, and therefore, had compassion for me. He gave me his treasures, objects within leather pouches, which brought both him and me fulfillment. My life too is spent. Fellow "searcher," pass these simple things to the next one seeking wisdom. I gave them to an orphan in a Bedouin caravan. **WHAT IS IN YOUR SIGHT, WILL BE IN YOUR MIND!**

PART TWO

TELESIS

ESTABLISHING AND VISUALIZING GOALS

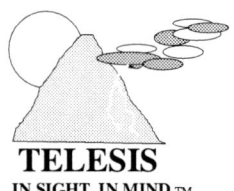

TELESIS
IN SIGHT, IN MIND ™

Establishing Goals

What Are They?
Where Do They Come From?
Why Does Telesis Work For You?
The Telesis Components.
Traps Of The Goal Setting Process!

VISUALIZATION

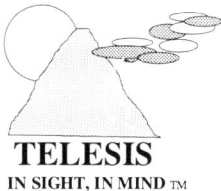

TELESIS
IN SIGHT, IN MIND ™

Goals, What Are They?

We all struggle with goals. What are they? We hear so much about them, but do we really know their purpose and reason behind our compulsion to have them? Many people use them as tools. Others have not discovered their value as tools.

To wish is to daydream, but since no effort is required, no reality is achieved. How are a wish and a goal different then? A goal is the manufactured product of thought, effort and planning with a particular date for its accomplishment, and just as importantly, an attitude of positive expectation.

To progress from desire to attainment of a particular trait, value, object, or situation, is often frustrating for those who have not experienced the actual process. Yes, there is a step by step process that must be followed.

What is this process? It will unfold page by page in the Telesis. Since we all learn things in different ways, it is, therefore, important to realize that we do not all learn the same way, at the same speed, or with the same interest or intensity. We do, however, learn easier, faster, with more interest, and remember longer those things we discover, create, manipulate, and sacrifice to obtain. The Telesis serves this purpose. It becomes the catalyst to activate the goal striving capability within you. It allows your creative mechanism to work for you automatically as you stimulate its operation and functioning by supplying images, feedback, reinforcement, and motivation for its operation.

TELESIS

The basic assumption of the *Telesis* is that **thoughts are blue prints for reality. Actions are the derivatives of thoughts. We move forward or backward because of the thoughts we think.** Just as a successful builder drafts a blue print and builds a structure on paper before building the structure in reality, we should discover the gift that allows us to mentally construct a blueprint of the actual goal or result we wish to achieve.

The *gift* we all have is that endowment given us at birth which inspires us to reach out and move forward. We are goal oriented. The purpose of the Telesis is to assist the participant in the process of self-investigation. When a person can define his purpose, plot a course, visualize the end result of his planning, and experience the satisfaction of deliberately succeeding, the word work takes on a different meaning.

The ability to act or make the choice is preferable to being acted upon or defaulting our life to others. We need to take control and responsibility for ourselves. To transform ourselves from the life of a caterpillar to the life of the butterfly is the challenge.

Experiment! "DO THE THING, AND YOU WILL HAVE THE POWER!" (Emerson)

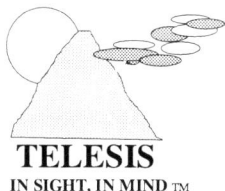

TELESIS
IN SIGHT, IN MIND ™

Goals, Where Do They Come From?

Our innate desire to achieve is a free gift at birth. Some societies try to destroy this gift. In this country of ours, we have the proper seed bed. As humans we have been endowed with this marvelous gift. In man, this gift is incredibly powerful when it is understood and controlled at will. This innate desire to seek out and want to improve is enhanced or diminished as we go through life. This gift operates with complete objectivity. It moves us toward those values, ideas, actions, circumstances, and attitudes that we think about. Thoughts are its source of fuel. Its fuel supply is endless.

When this gift is controlled, we move forward experiencing the good in life. When the power is without direction, it may be destructive to us. Some people succeed because they are able to channel the power correctly even though many do it unconsciously. Thus we say, *they are just naturally successful.*

We are happiest when we have something to work toward. The hope, the desire, the drive for improvement are all evidences of the gift within us. This gift tells us to reach out, take a chance on ourselves and hope for the best. A running tractor can plow a furrow, but it takes a driver to plow a straight furrow and give it purpose. We are constantly plowing furrows. However, most of us are preparing space for seeds sown for failure rather than plowing furrows preparing space for seeds of success. The challenge then is to take control. The Telesis will provide the control.

The successful achievement of any goal requires that a proper seed bed exist. In this great country of ours, the seed bed is freedom. Our

TELESIS

government doesn't restrict our movement. We are encouraged to explore the free market system. We can do amazing things when we are beneficiaries of a free society. Having a proper seed bed is necessary. Just as important, however, is having the proper motivation. **When interest fails, concentration wanes, and not much happens. The Telesis creates interest, focuses concentration, and makes things happen.**

When we cultivate our lives in a proper seed bed with the right motivation, we can do amazing things. Our thoughts are vectors toward destinations and actions. Our actions and circumstances are the off-spring of the thoughts we think. Thoughts are goals in miniature. They are conceived when present interest unites with emotion. Icons\pictures provide visualization, imprinting a "mental map." The power of the Telesis technique creates visualization that pulls us forward toward positive expectation and eventual reality acquisition. Remember, **In Sight, In Mind!**

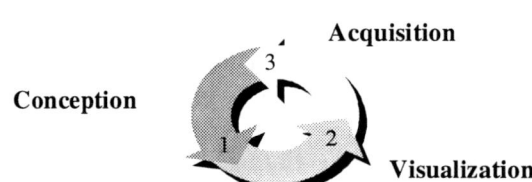

Conception — **Acquisition** — **Visualization**

"ALL THAT A MAN ACHIEVES AND ALL THAT HE FAILS TO ACHIEVE IS THE DIRECT RESULT OF HIS OWN THOUGHTS." (James Allen)

VISUALIZATION

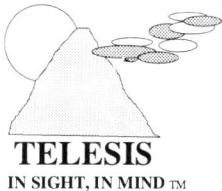

TELESIS
IN SIGHT, IN MIND ™

Why Does The Telesis Work For You?

The gift within each of us processes our thoughts even as we sleep. The fuel is consumed, energy is created and must be utilized, but may be wasted. This gift may be inefficient and out of control like a missile without a flight path and map programmed into its memory. How foolish we say to launch a missile without instructions and a picture of its target in its memory. Yet here we are attempting to navigate through life without any instructions, coordinates, map, or strategy for our own success. We all have this gift, yet we may lack the process to give us the direction to a particular path.

How does this gift function you ask? Surprisingly, its secret has been known for ages. We just don't take the time to profit from the experiences of those that have used it wisely. It operates below conscience awareness. It responds to a present need and moves us in that direction. What we think points the gift in a particular direction. **We move in the direction of the things we think about. I repeat, we move in the direction of the things we think about. Thought is the operative which controls this gift.** The necessity is to control this gift by what we think. The challenge is to control our thoughts. Accomplish this, and we have the power!

The Telesis harnesses the thoughts through appropriate stimuli of written words, visualization, creative genius, and imagination. All work together to form the mental framework upon which this gift can build a blueprint for the mind to follow. The **goals are worked on and completed successfully mentally, before they are actually achieved in reality. Many people experience this in their lives.**

TELESIS

This form of action is often defined as *mental practice*. Successful athletes, musicians, and others attest to its validity and usefulness. The Telesis becomes the organizer for this exercise in gaining control.

As you begin to explore this gift, be patient and don't try to force it. It can be a pleasant servant or become a ruthless taskmaster. It responds best when it knows the goal but is left alone to supply the means for its accomplishment. You supply the destination; it will find the proper path.

  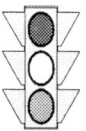

The worried man made an observation that changed his life forever. In taking a train from the East Coast to California, he noticed the engineer left the station when the first light changed from red to green. The engineer took all passengers safely to California one green light at a time. Once a light was passed, it was forgotten.

A man worries. Sometimes he actually WORRIES in advance. He IMAGINES unfavorable results and circumstances for himself. When making a decision, he WANTS to know everything. He WANTS to know everything that can go right. Human nature seems to force us to work on the problems first, rather than contemplating the possibilities. We become focused on the potential problems. We are derailed before we can visualize the success. **We should concentrate on the possibilities!**

VISUALIZATION

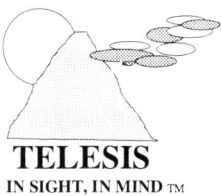

TELESIS
IN SIGHT, IN MIND ™

The Telesis Components

Mission Statement

The mission statement is a general **description of your philosophy, intentions, expectations, desires, or purpose.** It may be a paragraph or a page describing your purpose or intentions in any area.

Motivation

Motivation is an expansion of your mission statement. It may take a full page or even two. You decide! Describe in specific terms the concepts and ideas of your mission statement. Especially important is a description of positive admonitions. This is where you describe **why** you can succeed, and the **reasons** you can accomplish your hopes and dreams. Describe your success and receive strength and confidence from your accomplishments.

Personal Offering

Anything of value exacts a price. Be descriptive in explaining **the price you are willing to pay to accomplish your goals.** It may be time, TV, studying, patience, or whatever. This section is important. When you find you are lagging behind your expectations, review this section to see if you are still paying the price for the reward you expect.

Developmental Areas

Describe in this section your present base line (**how you see these areas of your life now**). Then describe **how you would like these areas to be**. Identify by yourself or with another person any problem areas, list possible alternatives, and the personal offering that may be required to facilitate the change. Consider your goals as they relate to the following areas:

Spouse, Family, Health, Finance, Education, Personal Growth, Relationships (areas that are important to you)

Visualizations

Since a picture is worth a 1000 words, this section becomes the foundation of the Telesis. **In this section you find pictures, or printed copy (in color as much as possible) that represent your specific goals in each of the above life areas.** Mental images and symbols of your goals provide a very powerful stimulus allowing the gift within you to begin searching for a path toward goal attainment. **The visualizations crystallize the mental-mapping process of your Telesis.** Organized as shown below, visual aids are placed as they relate to a given area of your life. Visuals of one goal goes on one page, another goal on the next and so on. On these pages also list the target dates for their accomplishments. This establishes a certain urgency and eliminates procrastination.

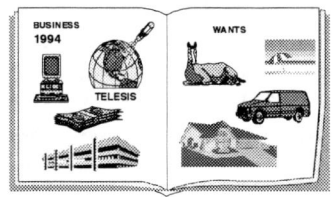

VISUALIZATION

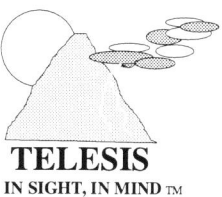

TELESIS
IN SIGHT, IN MIND ™

Traps Of The Goal Setting Process

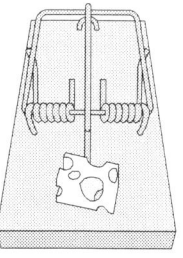

**PERPETUAL PREPARATION
THOUGHT WITHOUT ACTION
ACTION THAT IS UNPLANNED
THOUGHT WITHOUT OUR PRESENT INTEREST**

Continual and perpetual preparation can be a major problem in the goal setting process! Too often you can find yourself locked in a loop of being forever ready but never being able to precipitate action. You must be careful not to forget that goals must be fortified with action. Although the gift within you can automatically point the direction when you supply the goal, it cannot do the work or put forth the effort without the physical body.

There is a working relationship between the spiritual, the mental, and the physical. All are necessary; all are required; all must be implemented. THOUGHT AND ACTION are the combination. *Making it happen* and *letting it happen* are the catalysts for the results we seek.

There is an opposition in the process. The subconscious mind must not be forced. It should be free to explore the options and point the direction. This is where we *let it happen*. On the other hand, the conscious mind should *make things happen*.

To summarize, "faith without works is dead" or **goals without effort are wisps of smoke called wishes.** For the benefit of the subconscious, we should *let it happen* by thinking about the result we desire and let the subconscious direct us toward our goal. We should move forward anticipating success for the goal we seek. For the benefit of the conscious mind, we should take action to bring about the desired results by *making it happen*.

Sometimes we move our lives forward or backward in a certain direction because we try to please others or live up to the expectations others have of us. Instead we need to rediscover those early dreams and desires. We should rekindle and ignite our old flames of interest which were our early passions. <u>**Goals work best for us when they are realistic, optimistic, enthusiastic and have our present interest!**</u>

VISUALIZATION

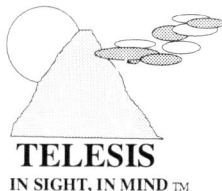

TELESIS
IN SIGHT, IN MIND ™

Personal Awareness

It's never too late to rediscover and implement action toward some unfulfilled desire or goal!

 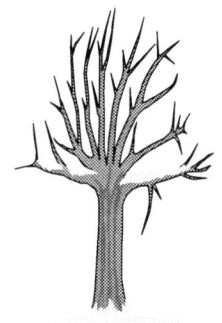

Whether we are in the spring, summer, autumn, or winter of our lives there is always time to realize our unfulfilled hopes and dreams. As long as there is sap in the tree it still lives! When we anticipate change in our lives it is often necessary to reflect upon our past successes. We are often too critical of our past performances. It is upon the foundation of our past successes that future growth and development is constructed! We can often use as a basis for our future development the following:

Steps Of Positive Self-Direction
Personal Seeds Of Success
A Personal Inventory

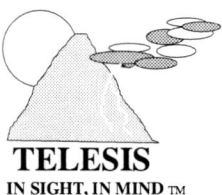

TELESIS
IN SIGHT, IN MIND ™

Personal Awareness

Steps Of Positive Self-Direction
Personal Awareness
Identification
Evaluation
Visualization
Monitor and Correction
Responsibility
Daily Practice

Personal Seeds Of Success
Childhood
Adolescence
Adulthood

A Personal Inventory
Personality
Interests
Attitude
Priorities
Environment
Values
Commitments

VISUALIZATION

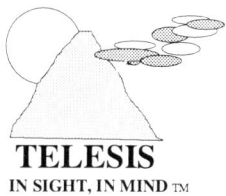

TELESIS
IN SIGHT, IN MIND ™

Steps of Positive Self-Direction

Personal Awareness

We may find ourselves at times unsettled, dissatisfied, confused, too comfortable, without change or challenges in our life, stagnant and impotent in our ability to move our lives forward.

Identification

We may discover a problem we desire to solve, a value we desire to acquire, a goal we desire to achieve, and a direction we desire to go.

Evaluation

We may contemplate solutions, opportunities, possibilities for success, and attempt to predict the outcome.

Visualization

We may begin to have mental images of the end results we hope to experience. We may actually see ourselves in possession of that which we desire with its accompanying emotions and feelings.

Monitor and Correction

We may even "keep score" and make adjustments as we move forward. A goal is best understood when it is fragmented. Break it down into daily, weekly, and monthly components which can be more easily absorbed by the mind and body.

Responsibility

We may even decide it is desirable to "affect circumstances" of our own choosing rather than be the recipient of "affected circumstances." Do we act or are we acted upon?

Daily Practice

We may realize that to become proficient in achieving our goals, a procedure, a plan, a new philosophy may be helpful. Learning how to effectively move toward self-direction may require just as much commitment as a piano student or golfer may require. Positive self-direction can become a learned skill through daily practice.

WE MUST HAVE A GOAL OR TARGET!

VISUALIZATION

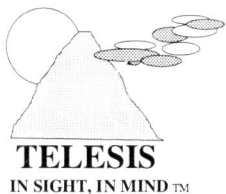

TELESIS
IN SIGHT, IN MIND ™

Personal Seeds Of Success

We are occasionally good at putting ourselves down or belittling our successes. It seems to come natural for some to diminish a sincere compliment by saying, "Ah, it was nothing." Success, however, must grow from something. Even success is germinated from a seed. Even if the seed is intangible, it still exists. You must identify your seeds of success. We are all unique. We are all different. We all have value. No one is valueless. Below recall your earliest times you were successful. Identify your seeds of success from the earliest past to the latest present. Most likely you will see that the pattern of your life has had many more successes than you thought. The purpose here is to assist you in recalling to the present, your seeds of success, so they can be nourished in such a way to move you forward, in accomplishing your desires or goals.

My Successes

Childhood

_____
_____
_____

Adolesence

_____
_____
_____

Adulthood

_____
_____
_____

TELESIS

Personal Inventory

The purpose here is to help you become aware of how you see yourself. It may be different from how others see you. This will help you to have goals that are consistent with your self image.

You may discover that to achieve what you truly desire you may have to make adjustments in your self image. By describing yourself in these areas you will begin to discover who you really are and if change is needed or observed in certain aspects of your life.

This information becomes your personal "wake-up" call. You may wish another person to fill this out as well. What you may find about yourself from others may be different than you would expect.

Personality (Describe yourself. Are you outgoing, timid, serious, carefree, or something else?)

_____
_____
_____
_____
_____

Interests (Describe what you enjoy doing.)

_____
_____
_____
_____
_____

Attitude (Describe how you think you are. This may be different from how you are perceived by others.)

_____
_____
_____
_____
_____

VISUALIZATION

Priorities (Describe what you devote the most time to: family, business, career, education, other.)
_____
_____
_____
_____
_____

Environment (Do you prefer indoors or outdoors, employee, entrepreneur?)
_____
_____
_____
_____
_____

Values (How do you value honesty, ethics, morals, relationships?)
_____
_____
_____
_____
_____

Commitments (loyalty, respect, sharing, giving, taking)
_____
_____
_____
_____
_____

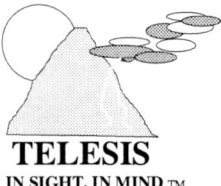

TELESIS
IN SIGHT, IN MIND ™

Life Management Areas

Nearly all aspects of one's life can be grouped into these four basic groups. You should classify your present goals and needs into these four groups and begin to prioritize them. Begin with those you have an interest in or those that require immediate attention. Don't overwhelm yourself, be selective.

For each major life area, describe briefly how you see this particular aspect of your life. Establish your *baseline*. Then describe briefly your *expectation* of the results for which you are striving. This establishes a starting point, gives direction, and implants your goal in a *seed bed*.

The following pages will help you organize this task. It may take several attempts to describe accurately your baseline and expectations for the mission statements, motivations, personal offerings, and visualizations for the four life management areas.

Establishing Our Present Position

Baseline
Expectation

VISUALIZATIONS

Personal Developmental Area

Spiritual
Health
Hobbies
Recreation
Relationships

Family Developmental Area

Spouse
Children
Trips
Vacations

Educational Developmental Area

Reading
Home Study
Seminars
College

Business Developmental Area

Plans
Objectives
Obstacles
Expansions
Employees
Employer

TELESIS
IN SIGHT, IN MIND ™
Establishing Our Present Position
Personal Management Area

Baseline (Describe the way things are in your personal life. Be brief, you will detail more later.)
_____
_____
_____
_____

Expectation (Describe briefly the way you would like things to be.)
_____
_____
_____
_____

Family Management Area

Baseline (Describe the way things are in your family life. Be brief, you will detail more later.)
_____
_____
_____
_____

Expectation (Describe briefly the way you would like things to be.)
_____
_____
_____
_____

VISUALIZATIONS

Education Management Area

Baseline (Describe the way things are in your educational life. Be brief, you will detail more later.)
_____
_____
_____
_____

Expectation (Describe briefly the way you would like things to be.)
_____
_____
_____
_____

Business Management Area

Baseline (Describe the way things are in your business life. Be brief, you will detail more later.)
_____
_____
_____
_____

Expectation (Describe briefly the way you would like things to be.)
_____
_____
_____
_____

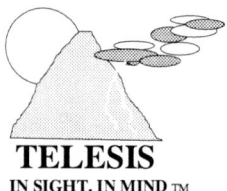

TELESIS
IN SIGHT, IN MIND ™

Personal Developmental Area

Goal and Mission Statement (State your goal, and then write your mission statement/purpose of your goal.)

_____
_____
_____
_____
_____
_____
_____
_____
_____
_____
_____
_____
_____

Motivations (State your reasons for the goal/desired improvement.)

_____
_____
_____
_____
_____
_____
_____
_____
_____
_____
_____
_____
_____

VISUALIZATIONS

Personal Offering (State what you are willing to sacrifice for your goal/desired improvement.)

_____
_____
_____
_____
_____
_____
_____
_____
_____
_____
_____
_____
_____

Visualization (Describe as vividly as you can your expectation about the outcome of your goal.)

_____
_____
_____
_____
_____
_____
_____
_____
_____
_____
_____
_____
_____

Gathering /Collecting Icons (When you see a picture/icon, in some magazine or other media that represents a particular goal, place it in a file corresponding to your developmental categories. These will be placed and organized in the visualization section of your Telesis. See page 72)

TELESIS

TELESIS
IN SIGHT, IN MIND ™

Action Plan Sequence And Keeping Score

Personal Management Area

Sequence First Things First   Obstacles To Overcome

1. _____ _____
2. _____ _____
3. _____ _____
4. _____ _____
5. _____ _____
6. _____ _____
7. _____ _____
8. _____ _____
9. _____ _____
10. _____ _____

Start Date   Completion Date

1. _____ _____
2. _____ _____
3. _____ _____
4. _____ _____
5. _____ _____
6. _____ _____
7. _____ _____
8. _____ _____
9. _____ _____
10. _____ _____

VISUALIZATIONS

        Desired Result   * Facilitating Stimulus

1. _____ _____
2. _____ _____
3. _____ _____
4. _____ _____
5. _____ _____
6. _____ _____
7. _____ _____
8. _____ _____
9. _____ _____
10. _____ _____

* The facilitating stimulus rewards you along the way. We all work harder if we are rewarded. It is important to reward yourself as you move forward (clothing, golf, vacation).

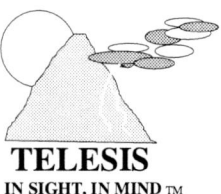

TELESIS
IN SIGHT, IN MIND ™

Family Developmental Area

Goal and Mission Statement (State your goal, and then write your mission statement/purpose of your goal.)

_____
_____
_____
_____
_____
_____
_____
_____
_____
_____
_____
_____

Motivations (State your reasons for the goal/desired improvement.)

_____
_____
_____
_____
_____
_____
_____
_____
_____
_____
_____
_____

VISUALIZATIONS

Personal Offering (State what you are willing to sacrifice for your goal/desired improvement.)

_____
_____
_____
_____
_____
_____
_____
_____
_____
_____
_____
_____

Visualization (Describe as vividly as you can your expectation about the outcome of your goal.)

_____
_____
_____
_____
_____
_____
_____
_____
_____
_____
_____
_____

Gathering /Collecting Icons (When you see a picture/icon, in some magazine or other media that represents a particular goal, place it in a file corresponding to your developmental categories. These will be placed and organized in the visualization section of your Telesis. See page 72.)

TELESIS

TELESIS
IN SIGHT, IN MIND ™

Action Plan Sequence And Keeping Score

Family Management Area

Sequence First Things First   Obstacles To Overcome

1. _____   _____
2. _____   _____
3. _____   _____
4. _____   _____
5. _____   _____
6. _____   _____
7. _____   _____
8. _____   _____
9. _____   _____
10. _____   _____

Start Date   Completion Date

1. _____   _____
2. _____   _____
3. _____   _____
4. _____   _____
5. _____   _____
6. _____   _____
7. _____   _____
8. _____   _____
9. _____   _____
10. _____   _____

VISUALIZATIONS

        Desired Result   * Facilitating Stimulus

1. _____ _____
2. _____ _____
3. _____ _____
4. _____ _____
5. _____ _____
6. _____ _____
7. _____ _____
8. _____ _____
9. _____ _____
10. _____ _____

* The facilitating stimulus rewards you along the way. We all work harder if we are rewarded. It is important to reward yourself as you move forward (clothing, golf, vacation).

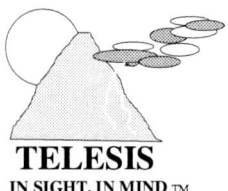

TELESIS
IN SIGHT, IN MIND ™

Education Developmental Area

Goal and Mission Statement (State your goal, and then write your mission statement/purpose of your goal.)

_____
_____
_____
_____
_____
_____
_____
_____
_____
_____
_____
_____
_____

Motivations (State your reasons for the goal/desired improvement.)

_____
_____
_____
_____
_____
_____
_____
_____
_____
_____
_____
_____
_____

VISUALIZATIONS

Personal Offering (State what you are willing to sacrifice for your goal/desired improvement.)

_____
_____
_____
_____
_____
_____
_____
_____
_____
_____
_____
_____

Visualization (Describe as vividly as you can your expectation about the outcome of your goal.)

_____
_____
_____
_____
_____
_____
_____
_____
_____
_____
_____
_____

Gathering /Collecting Icons (When you see a picture/icon, in some magazine or other media that represents a particular goal, place it in a file corresponding to your developmental categories. These will be placed and organized in the visualization section of your Telesis. See page 72.)

TELESIS

TELESIS
IN SIGHT, IN MIND ™

Action Plan Sequence And Keeping Score

Education Management Area

Sequence First Things First   Obstacles To Overcome

1. _____ _____
2. _____ _____
3. _____ _____
4. _____ _____
5. _____ _____
6. _____ _____
7. _____ _____
8. _____ _____
9. _____ _____
10. _____ _____

Start Date   Completion Date

1. _____ _____
2. _____ _____
3. _____ _____
4. _____ _____
5. _____ _____
6. _____ _____
7. _____ _____
8. _____ _____
9. _____ _____
10. _____ _____

VISUALIZATIONS

                Desired Result   * Facilitating Stimulus

1. _____ _____
2. _____ _____
3. _____ _____
4. _____ _____
5. _____ _____
6. _____ _____
7. _____ _____
8. _____ _____
9. _____ _____
10. _____ _____

* The facilitating stimulus rewards you along the way. We all work harder if we are rewarded. It is important to reward yourself as you move forward (clothing, golf, vacation).

Business Developmental Area

Goal and Mission Statement (State your goal, and then write your mission statement/purpose of your goal.)

_____
_____
_____
_____
_____
_____
_____
_____
_____
_____
_____
_____
_____

Motivations (State your reasons for the goal/desired improvement.)

_____
_____
_____
_____
_____
_____
_____
_____
_____
_____
_____
_____

VISUALIZATIONS

Personal Offering (State what you are willing to sacrifice for your goal/desired improvement.)

_____
_____
_____
_____
_____
_____
_____
_____
_____
_____
_____
_____
_____

Visualization (Describe as vividly as you can your expectation about the outcome of your goal.)

_____
_____
_____
_____
_____
_____
_____
_____
_____
_____
_____
_____
_____

Gathering /Collecting Icons (When you see a picture/icon, in some magazine or other media that represents a particular goal, place it in a file corresponding to your developmental categories. These will be placed and organized in the visualization section of your Telesis. See page 72.)

TELESIS
IN SIGHT, IN MIND ™

Action Plan Sequence And Keeping Score

Business Management Area

Sequence First Things First   Obstacles To Overcome

1. _____   _____
2. _____   _____
3. _____   _____
4. _____   _____
5. _____   _____
6. _____   _____
7. _____   _____
8. _____   _____
9. _____   _____
10. _____   _____

Start Date   Completion Date

1. _____   _____
2. _____   _____
3. _____   _____
4. _____   _____
5. _____   _____
6. _____   _____
7. _____   _____
8. _____   _____
9. _____   _____
10. _____   _____

VISUALIZATIONS

                Desired Result   * Facilitating Stimulus

1. _____ _____
2. _____ _____
3. _____ _____
4. _____ _____
5. _____ _____
6. _____ _____
7. _____ _____
8. _____ _____
9. _____ _____
10. _____ _____

* The facilitating stimulus rewards you along the way. We all work harder if we are rewarded. It is important to reward yourself as you move forward (clothing, golf, vacation).

TELESIS

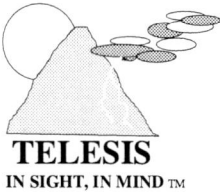

TELESIS
IN SIGHT, IN MIND ™

Rewards Of Telesis

Now that you have completed the basic task, are you finished? No! The goal book's (your Telesis) intent is to stimulate the creative force within you and provide the blueprint so that your gift may plot a path to your hopes and dreams. It provides a direction and means for you to evaluate your progress. If you see it through and use what you have created, **you should look to it daily to keep your thoughts centered and in focus.**

If the descriptive writing you are asked to do seems cumbersome to you, start with collecting the visuals that may represent what you perceive to be your interests. Place these related visuals on the same inserts shown on page 72. Begin to organize your life with visualizations. This is meant to be a growing process. Allow yourself some time for reflection. This project is designed to be flexible. Your Telesis will be on-going and as goals are achieved, replace them with new ones.

"Don't worry," just begin wherever you have the present interest. If you have completed some of the previous exercises, you have some idea of your planned destinations or goals.

Since we are seldom rewarded for the progress we make toward goal achievement, it is imperative that you reward yourself. When you have formulated and determined some of the things you wish to achieve, it is also enjoyable to place a **FS** (facilitating stimulus) on the **GOALS**. The **FS** are rewards to set for yourself. Work for the goal, but the **FS** is enjoyable too.

VISUALIZATIONS

A donkey will often walk toward a carrot when he cannot be moved any other way. The goal might be better communication with a spouse or friend. The **FS** might be a weekend of golf. The **FS** might be some new clothes. In the visualization section of your Telesis have a visual of your **FS** near the visual of the **GOAL**.

Make the **FS** a proper one. Its value should be appropriate for the effort needed to achieve the goal. At this junction in the process, you will discover that each step toward your goals can also be accompanied by periodic rewards for your effort.

The slaves of Egypt might have worked harder or more efficiently if they could have taken some of the bricks they made home with them. They could have traded them for food, clothing, and shelter. The value added for the Egyptians might have been a greater number of quality bricks.

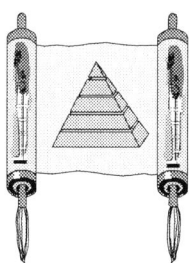

We may find ourselves working with extra effort when we know our efforts will be rewarded along the way. See previous pages, action plan sequence/keeping score, to list your **Facilitating Stimulus.**

TELESIS
IN SIGHT, IN MIND ™

Visualization Section

On adhesive pages in the Telesis binder, collect, through magazines, books, photographs, or any source available, representations of your goals for the respective *life management areas.* See page 106.

THIS SECTION BECOMES THE MOST POWERFUL PORTION OF TELESIS. It is here, **through daily review**, that your subconscious begins to work upon your goals. You most likely have done similar things by taping a picture or statement to your mirror or refrigerator. Now you will have a plan and system to follow.

This section is meant to be a **hands-on experience**. The value added for you is that it becomes your creation. It is not someone else establishing goals for you. You will change this section probably many times until you feel it is right. This flexibility is crucial to the metamorphic process of goal achievement.

If you have a computer, perhaps clip art programs will assist you. Magazines provide very good sources and they have brilliant colors. Once you have expectations 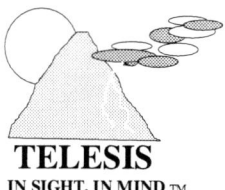 in mind and committed to paper, the search for visualizations is enjoyable and not difficult.

VISUALIZATIONS

The power of your Telesis project will be the results of what you have created! Truly, **"a picture is worth a 1000 words."** Consider the Chinese, Mayans, Egyptians, Annasazi, Incas, and of more recent date the Cuna Indians. The most effective way for you to convey to your subconscious mind what it is you wish it to accomplish is to give it an image or blueprint of what it should seek. An old Indian in September 1965 in Panama's San Blas Islands replied, *"We don't have a written language, but we have these pictographs which trigger back, as a mnemonic device, an old piece of our history."* Of his sketches and symbols he said, *"This one tells me we once had our history recorded and it was hidden in this mountain, covered over with jungle. It disappeared with the promise that it would be returned to us."*
(From Every Nation; Derin Head Rodriguez)

You must be able to specifically visualize yourself succeeding. You must be able to create a mental image of the goal. When you select pictures that represent your goals, your desires become a total picture, much clearer to your subconscious mind. A mental blueprint is then formed and a pathway selected that will move you forward.

Create mentally what it is you wish physically and select visuals that most accurately define and represent your goal. Each day as you look at these visuals you will reinforce your motivation. One visual can represent many pages of written word. It is more efficient and usually more stimulating as well.

<u>**Enjoy the creativity within you!**</u>

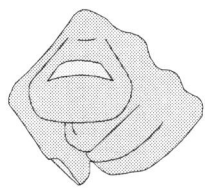

TELESIS

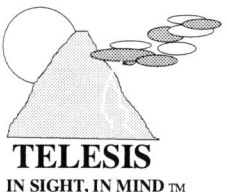

TELESIS
IN SIGHT, IN MIND ™

Placing And Organizing Icons

Everything that has preceded in Telesis to this point has been for the purpose of realizing that our minds are very active in the pursuit of a goal or target. It is our choice whether this process is random and without purpose or whether it is intelligently planned and directed, being organized for some meaningful reason. Below is an example of how your Telesis might look with Icons for the respective goal categories you have chosen.

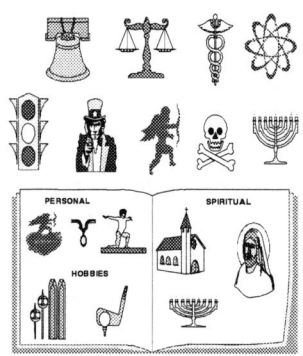

The samples above will serve to provide some idea of the placement of your respective icons within your Telesis visualizations pages. Once your Icons have been collected and organized in a similar manner as those demonstrated above, it becomes an easy process to review your goals at a glance. When you need occasional reinforcement return to your mission, motivation, and personal offering statements.

VISUALIZATIONS

SUMMATION

The Telesis process has as its foundation a phrase, IN SIGHT, IN MIND. The phrase, out of sight, out of mind, has been turned inside out just as you would a sock. Telesis theory suggests that we do move in the direction of those things which we think about and that have our present interest. Therefore, if we can control our thoughts effectively, we should become more efficient at moving toward the goals we set for ourselves.

The icons chosen as a result of working through the Telesis become the catalysts for moving us forward, almost automatically, as we supply to our mind the most perfect representation, in color and form, of what it is we would like our subconscious to accomplish. This icon becomes the goal or target. Telesis then acts like a "windows" program for the mind. Each icon chosen represents a vast array of information we process as we work through Telesis.

The mechanism in our brain that steers us toward our goals and desires is completely objective and it makes no value judgments. It is important to realize this. This mechanism simply asks for a goal or target upon which to expend energy. It is this mechanism in our possession that makes us unique as human beings. Some may be lead or controlled by this mechanism in the directions of their dominate thoughts to the distruction of themselves as well as their victims. A person's values is the "gyro" or governing factor for this mechanism. *We maintain or lose control because of our values. A person's values controls this mechanism.*

Consider the great men and women who because of their values and their ability to visualize, became great contributors to our society. Ben Franklin, Madam Curie, Louis Pasteur, Jonas Salk, and many others too numerous to present here. Let it be simply stated that these individuals are examples of the power generated by one who can

TELESIS

visualize an end result. Such individuals, seeing it mentally and holding the image, enable the image to be acted upon by the subconscious mechanism we all possess, its control being directed by proper values.

As one desires to make adjustments in his/her life, certain changes become inevitable. The changes can be pleasant or unpleasant, comfortable or uncomfortable, but, they will come. When we desire to move out of our comfort zones it also effects the comfort zones of significant others around us. When they see us change, they may feel comfortable or uncomfortable. Remember the lobster parable! The parables are for the purpose of dealing with the changes that we may have to make. Changes will always accompany new direction.

Remember, **Telesis means fulfillment, and to also intelligently plan and direct our behavior toward some worthwhile goal**. Lets us all strive to become "searchers" like *Anakrino*, and become "fulfilled" like *Telesis*.

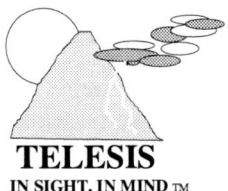

TELESIS
IN SIGHT, IN MIND ™

and

THANK YOU!

VISUALIZATIONS

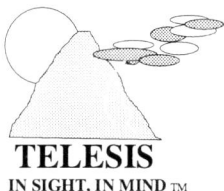

TELESIS
IN SIGHT, IN MIND ™

Larry Johanson
Box 687
Morgan, Utah
84050

1-801-829-6306
For information about speaking engagements, seminars,
and other Telesis products.